8/24/02

Dear Ann

Enjoy God's Plan.

Blessings!

GOD'S DIET
FOR HIS PEOPLE

By

[signature]

Mildred Dumas, N.D., C.N.H.P.

Library of Congress Catalog Number: 98-93744

Dumas Enterprises
1346 W. 155th Street
Gardena, California 90247

or

Dumas Enterprises
#20 Cottonwood Trace
Glen Carbon, IL 62043

Cover Design: Gene Brown

Editor: Geraldine Hayden

ISBN 0-9667905-0-2

CONTENTS

IN LOVING MEMORY OF

My Father

MR. JOE BEN DUMAS

who always supported me in all my
endeavors no matter how "off the wall" they
seemed.

and

My Beautiful, Talented
Daughter

D'AMBARA MERRIWEATHER

who died much too soon—before the world
had an opportunity to taste of her brilliance.

(If I had only known then what I know
now...)

*"My people are destroyed for lack of
knowledge:" Hosea 4:6*

ACKNOWLEDGMENTS

A lot of work is required in writing a book. I have many people to thank.

Special thanks go to: my mother, **Mrs. Mary Dumas,** who is sill hanging in there—ninety-three and counting—as I pour herbs and vitamins down her throat; **Geraldine Hayden,** for editing this book; **Gene Brown** for the cover design of **God's Diet for His People;** my **sisters, brothers, sisters-in-law,** and **brothers-in-law,** for trying to believe in me; my granddaughter, **Tricia,** for helping me with my business; my daughter, **JoEna,** for introducing me to the world of natural healing; **Dr. Barbara Flot** for the many workshops and meetings where I acquired a wealth of knowledge, and her husband, **Leonard** (her students' personal chef), for all the scrumptious food; my **Extended Herbal Family.** May God bless all of you.

FOREWORD

God's Diet For His People was written to provide nutritional information for all of God's people who are willing to open-mindedly read and consider the plausibility of its contents. I believe a book of this nature is needed and will be beneficial to many people by helping them change their lifestyles to become healthier and more productive members of society—if they so desire.

I was compelled to write this book because I am tired of seeing family members, friends, and acquaintances die before they really had a chance to live.

But...health is an individual thing. That means each of us has the responsibility of taking care of our own bodies. However, there is no need to fret. God has supplied us with all we need to perform this task, and we do not need to be doctors, nurses, or some other expert in the medical field. All we need do is read *THE BOOK,* and follow the laws, God's laws, as set down in it.

III

I do not believe God would have given us this magnificent piece of machinery in which to live without instructing us as to how to keep it functioning properly for the duration of its full-term existence upon this earth. I say full-term because thousands of people die prematurely every year of seemingly incurable conditions.

"The thief cometh not, but for to steal, and to kill, and to destroy: I am come that they might have life, and that they might have it more abundantly."
John 10:10.

It is this author's opinion that this means abundant life right here on earth as well as in Heaven. But How can one enjoy life to its fullest if one is in ill health? What can one do to assure oneself a life free of major, life-threatening conditions/diseases?

Do you leave your health in the hands of someone else, or do you take charge of your own body? If you have not done so already, perhaps this book will help you make a decision. God has given me this gift of knowledge. I herewith share it with you.

1

THE BEGINNING
GOD'S GREATEST
CREATION

CHAPTER ONE
The Beginning
(God's Greatest Creation)

"*And* God said, Let us make man in our image, after our likeness; and let them have dominion over the fish of the sea, and over the fowl of the air, and over the cattle, and over all the earth, and over every creeping thing that creepeth upon the earth.

So God created man in his own image, in the image of God created he him; male and female created he them." Genesis 1:26-27.

It is my opinion that since God gave man dominion over all the earth, God considered man to be the superior of all the creatures he had made. And in order for man to meet the challenge of his assigned responsibility, God would certainly give man what man needed to accomplish that task. He connected man's body systematically. At the top of one of man's systems, God put a computer that is so involved, so complex, so phenomenal, its capabilities are beyond man's wildest dreams.

The brain has approximately thirty billion cells. A minimum of 100 thousand chemical reactions take place in this intricate part of man every second.

Yet, man reportedly uses only ten percent of this wondrous computer. Why? Can you imagine (would you even dare to imagine) the kind of world we would have if we all used our brain to its fullest capacity? Or 90%, 75% or even 50%? Why would our creator equip us with an organ of such vast capabilities and not permit us to take full advantage of it? What can we do to unlock that untapped reservoir of potential? Is it something we are doing to block that blessing?

Man has certainly made a mess of the world with the little power he has been given. Only God knows what would happen if he were granted more. Could man be too smart for his own good? Perhaps man is so busy fighting—clamoring for power, prestige and money that he doesn't take the time to really listen to what God is trying to tell him.

"This is my commandment, That ye love one another as I have loved you." John 15:12.

The brain is a part of our...

Nervous System

The nervous system, our comunication network, can be compared to a city's communication system, linked by a central computer. This system provides the connection between the external world and our internal world. All of our senses: vision, hearing, smell, taste, and touch are a part of the nervous system network.

Stress can destroy this system. Stress is also related to nutrition because the fight/flight response steps up the metabolic process which increases the need for nutritional supplementation. Stress management is necessary to keep this system in good working order.

The Circulatory System

The circulatory system, the body's transportation system, transverses every tissue and organ in the body. It is an incredible network of about 60,000 miles of blood vessels. The center of this vast plumbing system is an eleven-ounce, fist-sized organ which pumps over 2,000 gallons of blood through its chambers each day. This is the center of life, the heart.

The life sustaining circulatory system must be properly cared for so it will not become clogged or restricted in its natural flow. Interruption of this flow could cause severe problems such as a heart attack.

Good nutrition plays an important role in the maintenance of this system.

The Digestive System

The body is built, repaired, and fueled by about a half ton of food per year. The food we eat must be digested, and assimilated in order to provide the life energy our bodies require. But if this system is not functioning properly, even the best nutrients do us little or no good.

Overeating, wrong food combining, drinking with meals, undue stress, and eating the wrong foods are some of the ways we abuse our digestive system.

The Intestinal System

The intestinal system, the body's waste disposal plant, is like a city's disposal plant. While the digestive system breaks down nutrients so they can be distributed throughout the body, the intestinal system absorbs waste products out of the body so that they can be excreted with indigestible food fiber.

The colon is affected by the types of foods we eat. People with diets high in refined foods like sugar and white flour and low-fiber foods like meat, eggs, and dairy products and low in high-fiber foods like fresh fruits, vegetables and whole grains are especially susceptible to intestinal problems.   Insufficient roughage leads to constipation or diarrhea.

When the colon is nutritionally supported, it is able to function at peak efficiency. When it is congested, it can promote illness and disease.

(Natural healers point out that death and disease begin in the colon.)

The Glandular System

The glandular system, the body's thermostat, works like a thermostat in any heating system. It controls the body's temperature. This system also regulates basic drives and emotions, promotes growth and sexual identity, assists in the repair of broken tissue, and helps to generate energy.

This system functions properly when it has ample stores of minerals, particularly trace minerals. Eating foods rich in trace minerals will help to nutritionally support the glandular functions of the body.

The Immune System

The immune system, the body's security system, is like the security forces of a city. It continually monitors the body for anything that is out of place. If it discovers something that challenges the well-being of the body, it dispatches appropriate defense mechanisms.

Some call the immune system, the sixth sense. It is capable of recognizing viruses and bacteria that the brain does not. It then converts that information into hormones that go to the brain and activate the immune process to destroy them. This system utilizes all the body's various systems when the body's well-being is challenged. Environmental pollutants, improper diet, other harmful habits such as smoking, and improper rest are some of the things that can reduce the immune system's ability to protect the body.

A balanced diet is the most important consideration in maintaining a healthy immune system.

The Respiratory System

The respiratory system, the body's oxygen supplier, is essential to the growth and movement of the body. By supplying oxygen, this system enables the body to produce energy.

The lungs are the center of the respiratory system. We are all born with a pair of bright, healthy, pink lungs. But an adult with a smoking habit and living in a city has dull pink-gray lungs with black patches.

The respiratory tract is especially vulnerable to particles floating in the air. It is estimated that city dwellers ingest as many as 20 trillion particles of foreign matter per day. The respiratory system has several ways of dealing with this problem: the cough and sneeze reflexes. They are essential to life, as they keep the passageways of the lungs clear of foreign matter.

It is essential that we maintain healthy lungs by breathing unpolluted air as much as possible and by supplying the body with good nutrition.

The Urinary System

The urinary system, the body's water treatment plant, is like a city's water treatment plant that assures its residents of a continual supply of fresh, pure water.

Our urinary system passes the water within our body through a filtration process in order to maintain a clean supply of body fluids that the different systems can utilize.

The kidneys, an integral part of this system, regulate the amount of water, acids and salts in the body and ensure that the body does not poison itself. About 300 pints of water are filtered in the kidneys each day. When there is too much fluid in the body, the kidneys excrete more water, and when there is not enough, they conserve water.

Potassium and sodium are crucial to the fluid balance in the body. The best way to get the potassium you need without the extra sodium is to eat more unprocessed, natural foods.

The Structural System

The structural system, the framework for the body, gives the body the same kind of support a building needs to withstand stresses and strains. This system is what gives the body form and the ability to move about. Without it, the body would collapse under its own weight. It also houses all the other systems of the body and protects them from the outside environment.

Calcium is most important for the proper functioning of this system. The body is constantly using calcium from the diet to replace old bone tissue with new tissue. When the calcium supply in the blood is low, the body takes calcium back from the bones without replacing it. Calcium is required in the bones to maintain health, strength, and hardness.

Consequently good nutrition, with a healthy supply of minerals, is needed for a healthy structural system.

All of the body's systems work synergistically to keep the body in a balanced state (homeostasis). Toxic overload can cause a breakdown of the systems. (If you noticed, all of the systems can be supported by proper nutrition—diet.)

The Toxic Stress Cycle In The Human Body—The National Association Of Certified Natural Health Professionals:

- The digestive system is stressed by depleted food, poor food combinations, water with meals, pollutants, additives, preservatives, improper chewing and poor mental attitude.
- The colon is affected by the undigested food and becomes toxic.
- The liver and gallbladder are the first to be affected by the toxic colon.
- The kidneys and bladder are then affected.
- The lungs are toxified by kidney weakness.

- The circulation is the next to be affected.
- The heart and spleen are then affected.
- The muscle and soft tissue are next to be affected.
- The spine area is then affected.
- The brain and nerves are affected.
- The endocrine glands are the last to be affected.

To bring about restoration, the body heals in the reverse order of the above.

And now, let us take a look at God's diet plan for His people, as this author believes is set down in *The Book.*

2

GOD'S DIET PLAN
As Set Down In
"The Book"

CHAPTER TWO
**God's Diet Plan As Set Down
In
The Book**

*"And God said, let us make man
in our image, after our likeness..."
Genesis 1:26.*

And when God made this magnificent
machine called man, He also gave it everything it needed to stay in good operating
condition for many years.

Before the fall, Adam and Eve had
eternal life, so everything they ate had life.
In the Garden of Eden, they ate seed-bearing

foods that came mostly from trees. After the fall, God added other kinds of vegetation to their diet.

"And God said...Behold, I have given you every herb bearing seed, which is upon the face of all the earth, and every tree, in the which is the fruit of a tree yielding seed; to you shall be for meat." Genesis 1:29.

And He did not forget the other creatures He had made.

"And to every beast of the earth, and to every fowl of the air, and to every thing that creepeth upon the earth, wherein there is life, I have given every green herb for meat; and it was so." Genesis 1:30.

"He causeth the grass to grow for the cattle, and herb for the service of man; that he may bring forth food out of the earth." Psalm 104:14.

"If ye be willing and obedient, ye shall eat the good of the land." Isiah 1:19.

It appears, to this author anyway, that God gave man and beast the same foods to eat—not one another.

Through the foregone verses, and many others in the Bible, our Father teaches us that there is healing and the possibility of longevity through the consumption of seed-bearing foods and the use of herbs for medicine. He knew that the properties He placed in the leaves and bark of the trees would build healthy bodies by renewing cells, cleansing the blood, and rejuvenating tissues and organs.

"And the Lord God formed man of the dust of the ground, and breathed into his nostrils the breath of life; and man became a living soul." Genesis 2:7.

Since man is made from the soil, and the same chemical elements are found in man as in the soil, it is easy to understand that food that comes from the soil would be the perfect food for man to consume.

God makes no mistakes. ·

With the advent of modernization, i.e., the cook stove (cooking—unless lightly steamed—removes the life from food rendering it, in most cases, useless to the body), man began to change his dietary habits to his own detriment.

But, even today with all the toxins, poisons, pesticides, herbicides, and pollution, just as a car is capable of being operable for over 200-300 thousand miles if it is properly maintained, the human body is capable of living in a healthy, productive, active state for at least 120-150 years—if it is cared for properly.

Some of you might ask, "Why would I even want to live that long? What would be the purpose?" To that, I say, why not? You just might find a purpose. Who knows what God has in store for any of us?

For those of you who might be thinking *I would be useless, sick, hurting, decrepit, feeble, absent-minded, dried-up, wrinkled, dependent, etc.* Not so. That is one of the reasons for this book—to let people know that simply because one lives one-hundred or more years, he/she does not have to be all/if any of those things. Who says one cannot be a viable, constructive, and useful person in his or her society simply because one is over retirement age—as set down by man? If one is sick and infirmed, at any age, one is unable to function at one's fullest capacity.

So, what is the proper way to care for our bodies? In my opinion, diet is the key. And the key to the proper diet for the body is found in *the book, the Holy Bible.*

"...to you it shall be for meat."

God was speaking of the fruit of the tree not the pig, cattle, fowl, rabbit, deer, opossum, raccoon, etc.

(Yes, opossum and raccoon. My father was an avid hunter. He would kill these creatures, and my mother would cook them—surrounded by sweet potatoes. My family enjoyed this delicacy for many years.)

"Moreover ye shall eat no manner of blood, whether it be of fowl or of beast, in any of your dwellings." Leviticus 7:26.

"...I will even set my face against that soul that eateth blood and will cut

him off from among his people. For the life of the flesh is in the blood..." Leviticus 7:10-11.

One's body is only as clean as one's blood. It flows from head to toe, carrying life-sustaining or life-threatening properties to every cell and organ in the body. Therefore, when we eat the flesh of the animals, we are subjected to all of the diseases the animals may have, plus the chemicals in the food that has been fed them and the injections they receive.

Everything we eat affects our blood, and so it is with all of God's creatures.

"...For the life of the flesh is in the blood... flesh with the life thereof, which is the blood thereof, shall ye not eat." Genesis 9:3-4.

Throughout history, there have been people who sensed that eating the flesh of animals was not in keeping with striving toward the goal of bringing peace to the world. One great philosopher asked how we could expect to enjoy ideal conditions on earth when we are, in fact, the living graves of slaughtered beast. Another said that the time will surely come when men will finally acknowledge that the murder of animals is as much a crime as the murder of men.

"Meat reduced man's life span from Methuselah's nine hundred sixty-nine years to Noah's descendants' approximately one hundred forty-eight years or less."—God's Nutrition Laws, Zoe Ministries, Los Angeles, California.

If this is so, meat is a mighty deterrent of life. Is eating meat worth giving up thirty to forty years of your life?

Many stand on faith and prayer for healing of various diseases that threaten their lives. Then they become dismayed and discouraged when that healing does not come. This author believes their healing does not come, because they do not heed God's dietary and nutritional laws. Think about it. Why should God do for you what you could do for yourself?

I am not saying that God is not still in the healing business. He is, as God's children know all too well.

I have a cousin who was healed of cancer. The doctors gave her six months to live. She did not give up, however, and continued to take the drugs they prescribed for her. But she said the medicine made her feel worse than the disease itself. Being a child of God, she was in constant prayer for her healing. One day, she flushed the medicine that was making her so miserable down the toilet and put everything in the Master's hands. Nineteen years later, she is still living and, and as far as she knows, her body is cancer free. She feels wonderfully blessed.

But...I had a daughter to die at the tender age of twenty-six, and a niece to die at twenty-two. They both succumbed to different forms of cancer. They and others were praying for their healing, but, for some reason, God chose not to heal their bodies. Why? We'll never know.

However, I met a woman a few years ago who has been living with the form of cancer that killed my daughter—longer than my child was on this earth—by controlling the disease with herbs. I also met a man who said his doctors had given him six months to one year to live because of lung cancer that had metastasized to other parts of his body. But instead of accepting this grim prognosis, he decided to do something to try to help himself. He knew someone involved with herbs and alternative methods of healing. He went on an herbal program. It was eight years later that I met him. He was still alive and well, and, as far as he knew, free of cancer.

Would these two people also be dead now if they had not taken the alternative route to combat this disease? Only God knows the answer to that question.

Since you just might be one of the cases He would choose not to heal if you were to contract one of the many killer diseases that plague our society today, don't you think you should do all you can to keep from contracting a disease, or, if you already have one, do what you can to stop the progression of that disease? I trust you will.

   "My people are destroyed for lack of knowledge." Hosea 4:6.

   "God will not bypass the laws that He set up and grant believers divine healing as long as they continue to bring the illness upon themselves by completely ignoring and/or abusing His nutritional laws!"— Zoe Ministries, Los Angeles.

   God's diet plan for us is written.

   Do we dare argue with *the book?*

   We go to church, sing, shout, listen to—and identify with—the preacher. We read our Bibles and strive to live according to God's word. How, then, did we miss our dietary plan when it is there like all the rest? Or, do some people just choose to disregard it because they simply like the taste of the foods they have grown accustomed to eating and would rather die than alter that life-threatening diet?

But that is one's right as custodian of one's own body—to eat what one pleases, or what pleases one's palate. But is it worth the pain and grief that it causes—not only to the one who suffers and dies from some debilitating disease but to loved ones who are left behind, most of the time, devastated and confused, especially if that person is in the prime of his or her life—or has not even really begun to live like my daughter and my niece? I think not.

As Christians, we must be concerned about what we put into our bodies. There is one especially good reason:

"What? Know ye not that your body is the temple of the Holy Ghost which is in you, which ye have of God, and ye are not your own?" Corinthians 6:19.

Therefore, since our bodies are the temples of the Holy Ghost, should we not be concerned about desecrating God's temple? Would you clean your house if you knew Jesus was coming for a visit? Of course, you would. You would not ask Him to sit in a filthy room. Why, then, would you ask

God to dwell in a nasty, toxic-laden, polluted body by feeding it substances that it is incapable of utilizing, causing this poisonous condition, that contributes to lowering of awareness, and loss of energy and productivity—a condition that is subject to destroy your body prematurely? Why not offer Him an improvement in health—mind and body? It might not be easy but it can be done.

We are what we eat. God is good and has provided us with all we need to maintain/regain good health.

Everyone is responsible for his or her own health. What we do with our bodies is our choice, and how we feed and take care of our bodies will determine the kind of health we will have—good (body balanced/ homeostasis) or bad (diseased). It is each person's responsibility to learn what fuel is good for the building, nourishment, and over-all upkeep of his or her most precious possession—and that which is not.

The book addresses this concern also.

"... They shall also make gardens, and eat the fruit of them." Amos 9:14.
"In the sweat of thy face shalt thou eat bread..." Genesis 3:19.
"... the Lord God sent him forth from the garden of Eden, to till the ground from whence he was taken". Genesis 3:23.

Organically grown foods (without the pesticides, herbicides, fertilizers, etc. and being grown in devitalized, mineral-depleted soil) is the best food for the body to consume. Our ancestors grew this kind of food before man decided to help things along by adding his touches to an already good thing that did not need any fixing.

Planting one's own organic garden in this day and age (tilling the ground) is obviously not feasible for most people, but there are health food stores that carry organically grown fruits and vegetables, whole grain products, etc. that one can incorporate into one's diet. All that is necessary for our bodies to be strong and healthy so that we may enjoy life to its fullest—without pain or disease that hamper our productivity can be found even in this day and age.

It is up to us to make the effort.

We must remember that if our bodies are sick, we cannot even serve God the way we should. An unhealthy person cannot function properly physically or mentally, thus all of the energy the sick/diseased person can generate is focused on his or her illness and trying to get well.

Look at the sick list in your church bulletin. How many members of your church family are away from church because of some illness? Approximately how many funerals are held at your church annually? Church members gone on to the great beyond, and most of them probably prematurely, because they were ignorant of God's law.

Who among us should be sick? God intended for His people to be healthy or He would not have provided us with grains, seeds, nuts, fruits and vegetables—substances that can help the body heal itself even when it is plagued with killer diseases such as AIDS, Alzheimer's Disease, Cancer, Stroke, Diabetes, Heart Disease, and Rheumatoid Arthritis.

Nearly all of these diseases are preventable. Our diet, lifestyle habits, and environment are all involved in generating these conditions in the body.

Unless we become victims of accidents, crime, or some other disaster that sometimes take our lives, our bodies should not be dying after fifty, sixty, seventy, eighty, ninety, or even one-hundred years of living.

And... if God made our bodies—and I am sure we all believe that to be so—who would know better than the creator of this intricate structure how to take proper care of it?

Good nutrition = a healthy body. Good nutrition affects how one looks and feels. Good nutrition determines how the body performs—physically, mentally, and spiritually (body, soul, and spirit).

Good nutrition comes from the ingestion of real food. Real food is **material that can be incorporated into and become a part of the cells and fluids of the body.** Real food is an edible substance in its natural state or as close to it as possible. Non-food items contain **useless or harmful ingredients:** i.e., **sugar,** a substance that is constantly overly consumed by millions of Americans daily. *(Sugar lies in the stomach and churns. After being in this nice, warm place for approximately ten to twelve hours, it ferments and becomes alcohol. Have you ever felt intoxicated and wondered why?)*

Good health is based upon a few essentials: pure water and air, healthy food, rest, exercise, and low stress.

You may think that in this day and age, with all of the crime and corruption (from the White House on down) and all the problems of just trying to live a decent, honest life from day to day, living a life without stress is virtually impossible. Yet we must try to accomplish just that in order to live a pain and disease-free life. With

God's help and the proper nourishment for the body, in spite of the chaos about us, we still might be able to manage a healthy lifestyle, including one with low stress.

The world is changing daily, and most of the time, change is challenged, if for no other reason than that it is different. There are many people who hate change and will do just about anything to prevent it, or, if not in a position to prevent it, they simply refuse to adjust their lives accordingly—until they are forced to do so (*as I was to leave my comfortable typewriter and use this complicated computer*).

Every advancement that has ever been made by the human race has met with challenge. These advancements have had to overcome the old order of things. Because the old order was indeed the makeup of the minds of a certain period, advancement could only come as the result of a mental revolution. People were taught to see things differently. They learned that progress did not mean the universe had to be destroyed. They acquired a new view of things, and soon realized that change, sometimes, is better, and that it is not good, sometimes, to resist change simply because of fear of the unknown.

So it is with nutrition.

Would a fair-minded individual not want to sift through, test, and give change a fair chance before completely rejecting it?

"My people are destroyed..."

Educate yourself. You will be glad you did.

In spite of ourselves and all of our objections, unless we are brain dead, we never stop learning.

Learning about your body and which dietary habits can hurt you and under-standing why certain substances found in your diet are harmful to your body can mean the difference between life and death.   This new-found knowledge will make it easier for you to change your dietary habits.

Satan, our adversary, is on the war-path trying to destroy us anyway he can, which includes undermining our health, and especially that of those who love the Lord. Satan knows that if a body is tired, distressed, diseased and diminished, it will not be capable of effective service to our Lord. When a body is infirmed, not only is that person weak physically, but his or her mental capacity is also diminished. How can we serve the Lord when our bodies are sick and our minds are consumed with trying to get well? But...

"...When he speaketh a lie, he speaketh of his own; for he is a liar, and the father of it." John 8:44.

Saints, it is time we got serious about our bodies. God did not create these magnificent structures, the temples in which He abides, for us to just dress them up in fine clothes, beautify, abuse, and stuff with anything simply because it satisfies our taste buds. If He went to the trouble of providing us with the proper foods to feed His greatest creation, should we not be obedient enough to utilize them?

This author thinks so. Otherwise, disease and premature death shall continue to follow us all the days of our lives.

I do not believe that was God's intention for us. After all, He is a kind and merciful God. Is He not? Hurting, suffering, pain, and disease are—in my opinion—not acts of kindness and mercy.

Just imagine how wonderful it would be to live a long, healthy, pain-free life, and simply go to sleep—your body maybe a little tired and weary from many years of wear and tear, but not filled with disease and hurting beyond belief—then awaken in the Master's arms in the beauty of all His glory.

What a marvelous day that would be! Don't you think? And you would have gone on to meet the Master feeling good and happy about the life you had lived, not glad it was over because of all the misery, pain, and suffering of some wasting, debilitating, ravishing disease that took your energy and your will to live.

Wouldn't that be the perfect conclusion to this earthly life?

Now...let us take a look at some of the diseases/conditions/bad habits that are so rapidly ravishing/killing the bodies of so many of God's children.

3

KILLER/
OTHER DISEASES
AND CONDITIONS
That Are Ravishing
And
KILLING
The Bodies Of
So Many Of
God's Children

CHAPTER THREE

Killer/Other Diseases/
Conditions

"Men dig their graves with their own teeth and die more by those instruments than the weapons of their enemies."
—Thomas Moffett, 1600 A.D.

This author's interpretation of what Mr. Moffett meant was, *we don't catch diseases, but rather create them by breaking down the natural defenses in our bodies according to the way we eat.* I would like to add to that, *the substances we drink and the way we choose to live our lives.*

What we ingest either keeps the body fit and healthy or eventually destroys it. Many of the foods we eat today wear the body out attempting to digest them, because they are too heavy or have the wrong properties in them. Therefore, the body is not equipped to easily digest them. The body was designed to digest chemically free, raw fruits and vegetables. Attempting to digest anything else, especially over a long period of time, will result in eventual breakdown of the system, exposing the body to all kinds of trauma and disease, such as the following diseases that take their toll on the body and kill thousands of people every year.

HEART DISEASE
(Number one killer)

A heart attack occurs when the supply of blood to a part of the heart muscle has been cut off. When the heart muscle is deprived of blood, the muscle cells suffer irreversible injury and die. Depending on how much of the heart muscle has been affected, the heart attack victim suffers disability and sometimes death.

Disorders of the heart are often far in the advanced stages before they become symptomatic. Approximately twenty-five percent of heart attack victims have no prior warning.

Some Causes Of Heart Attack
- Atherosclerosis (hardening of the arteries) is primary cause
- Cigarette smoking
- High blood pressure
- High blood cholesterol
- Alcoholism
- Sedentary lifestyle (little or no exercise/ couch potato lifestyle)
- Stress
- Diabetes
- Obesity

Most of the above conditions are diet related.

Statistics show that the United States leads the world in death rates from heart (cardiovascular) disease. Reportedly, over sixty million Americans currently suffer from this ailment, and over 550,000 die from it annually.

It is obvious, to this author anyway, that conventional medicine is failing in its fight against heart disease. But, there is an option: the natural approach/ alternative medicine/God's medicine.

Many health care professionals who practice alternative methods of healing are opposed to costly, complicated, and oftentimes dangerous drugs—and surgery. They prefer to work with the alternatives, that are much safer, to correct the biochemical and nutritional imbalances that can greatly affect the functioning of the heart.

Your heart is the most important muscle in your body. It is imperative that obstruction to this muscle is prevented.

CANCER
(Second Leading Cause Of Death)

Cancer. Just hearing the word is frightening and unnerving. Cancer is a disease that causes healthy cells to stop functioning and maturing properly. These cells begin to multiply, become parasitic, and may develop their own network of blood vessels that siphon nourishment away from the body's blood supply. If unchecked, this process will eventually lead to the formation of cancerous tumors. The cancer can also spread to other parts of the body, eventually poisoning the patient with toxic by-products.

Cancer is almost always fatal. According to Alternative Medicine: The Definitive Guide, it claims more than half a million Americans annually.

With this disease claiming so many lives, the search for a cure continues.

But... there is hope.

"And by the river upon the bank thereof, on this side and on that side, shall grow all trees for meat...and the

fruit thereof shall be for meat, and the leaf thereof for medicine." Ezekiel 47:12.

Some Causes Of Cancer
- Diet
- Smoking
- Environmental toxicity
- Environmental radiation
- Contaminated water
- Oxygen free radicals
- Oxygen deficiency
- Stress
- Dental hygiene

Let us briefly explore the above causes of cancer.

Diet. Diet plays a key role in good or bad health. A diet consisting largely of organically grown fresh fruits, vegetables, and whole grains, with little or no fat or meat is highly recommended.

Smoking. Smoking not only causes lung cancer but also cancer of the head, mouth, vocal cords, throat, kidneys, stomach bladder, cervix, pancreas, tongue, and lip. Smoking accounts for an estimated 350,000 deaths annually. Secondary smoke is also dangerous.

Environmental Toxicity. Toxic chemicals are found almost anywhere: in the home, work place, the air...

Environmental Radiation. A higher incidence of leukemia and brain tumors are linked to exposure to electrical power plants, fields, power lines, etc. Sitting/standing closer than six feet to the television or microwave is also dangerous.

Contaminated Water. Water supplies throughout the United States are tainted with toxic chemicals, heavy metals, parasites, pesticides, and other contaminants that have been linked to cancer.

A good water treatment system may solve this problem. For information on water treatment systems, send stamped, self-addressed envelope to:

M. D.'s Herbs For Life
1346 W. 155th Street
Gardena, CA 90247

Oxygen Free Radicals. Generated by toxic pollution, tobacco smoke, nuclear and ultraviolet radiation, and other substances. They attack and destroy the membranes that surround the cells, leaving the body vulnerable to cancer promoters.

Oxygen Deficiency. Cancer cells cannot exist in an oxygen-rich environment.

Stress. Severe stress can reportedly trigger cancer.

Dental Hygiene. According to Dr. Cass Igram in his book, Eat Right To Live Long, Oral hygiene is a critical component of cancer prevention. He states that infections in the mouth can weaken the immune system throughout the body and spread to other body tissues.

STROKE
(Reportedly The Third Leading Cause Of Death)

A stroke is a severe occurrence in the body in which there is a blockage of blood to a part of the brain resulting in damage to that particular part of the brain. Approximately thirty percent of strokes are fatal, approximately thirty percent result in partial loss of functions, and approximately thirty percent recover.

Some Causes Of Stroke
- High blood pressure (Hypertension)
- Thickening of lining of arteries
- Smoking
- Recent heart attack
- Elevated blood fats
- Diabetes
- Oral contraceptives
- History of damaged heart valve

Most of the conditions listed above are diet related.

AIDS
(Acquired Immune Deficiency Syndrome)

AIDS is a disease that is caused by a virus that attacks, and results in the complete degeneration of, the immune system. This virus avoids detection by the immune system by hiding inside the T-cells. It attaches itself to the chromosomes of the cell, and replicates without opposition. The newly produced viruses then go on to attack other T-cells, until the body has virtually 1. defenses left.

Some Known Causes Of AIDS
- Candidiasis (yeast or fungal growth)
- Chemicals (pesticides, herbicides, etc.)
- Immunosuppressive Drugs (given to cancer patients, organ donor recipients, etc.)
- Parasites (animals that invade body and live off host—most enter in/on foodstuffs)
- Stress

AIDS is still an enigma, and possible cures are still being sought. Most people think this disease is an automatic death sentence because most people who contract it do die. However, it does not have to be.

"My people are destroyed for lack of knowledge." Hosea 4:6.

We, in the alternative medicine field, believe that all diseases, if determined and properly treated in time, are reversible. This includes AIDS.

CIRRHOSIS OF THE LIVER
(Chronic Liver Disease)

Cirrhosis of the liver is a degenerative inflammatory disease that results in hardening and scarring of liver cells. The liver becomes unable to function properly due to the scarred tissue which prevents the normal passage of blood through the liver.

The death rate for this disease is approximately 30,000 a year.

Some Causes Of Liver Disease

- **Alcoholism** (chief cause, should be strictly avoided)
- Hepatitis
- Parasites
- Malnutrition
- Chronic inflammation
- Congestive heart failure

DIABETES

Diabetes mellitus, commonly known simply as diabetes, is a chronic degenerative disease caused by a lack of, or resistance to, the hormone, insulin, that is essential for the proper metabolism of blood sugar (glucose). Diabetics are either unable to produce insulin, or their cells have become resistant to insulin, and they are unable to move glucose from the bloodstream to the cells. Consequently, their bodies cannot maintain a normal blood glucose level.

Management of this disease is a day-by-day, hour-by-hour venture.

There are two types of diabetes.

Type I Diabetes

Type I diabetes is known as juvenile-onset or insulin-dependent diabetes. This type of diabetes usually begins in childhood and is usually caused by viral infections. It may also be a genetic disorder.

Type II Diabetes

Type II diabetes, also known as adult-onset or non-insulin-dependent diabetes, usually occurs in middle age. This type of diabetes is usually caused by poor diet, obesity, allergies to various foods, viral infections, and stress.

HIGH BLOOD PRESSURE
(Hypertension)

High blood pressure, also known as hypertension, is one of the most common—and the most serious and chronic—adult illnesses. It is a disease that involves the heart and the arteries that carry fresh blood to every part of the body. When blood cannot flow easily through vessels, pressure increases. This disease does its damage silently over a period of years.

Approximately 60 million Americans suffer from this illness. It is considered a major killer.

Some Causes Of High Blood Pressure
- Poor diet
- Obesity
- Lack of exercise
- Undue stress
- Smoking
- Alcohol consumption

OSTEOPOROSIS

Osteoporosis means porous bones. When bones become too porous, they break easily. Osteoporosis is a disabling disease affecting an estimated twenty-five million Americans (mostly women). Over forty-five thousand women die each year from this disease. It is painful and disfiguring.

Some Causes Of Osteoporosis
- Poor diet
- Insufficient exercise
- Not enough calcium in diet
- Decrease in levels of estrogen
- Decrease in levels of progesterone

Some Foods Reported To Promote Osteoporosis
- Processed foods
- Soft drinks
- Caffeine
- High protein foods
- Sugar
- Salt
- Red meat
- Fat
- Alcohol

Other Factors To Consider
- Aging too inactively
- Loss of sex hormones at menopause
- Family history
- Delicate bone structure
- Underweight

- Alcohol consumption
- Cigarette smoking
- Use of antibiotics (that deprive the body of Vitamin K which is needed in the building of bone)
- Fluoride
- Northern European heritage
- Fair skin
- Red or blond hair

ARTHRITIS

Arthritis is an inflammation of the joints surrounding tendons, ligaments, and cartilage. It can affect virtually every part of the body: knees, feet, fingers, back, shoulder, etc. The effects range from slight pain to crippling and disability. There are three types of this disease.

Osteoarthritis. A degenerative condition of the weight-bearing joints such as the knees, hips, and spine. Chronic irritation of the joints is the main contributing factor. Older people are more prone to have this form of arthritis than others.

Rheumatoid Arthritis. A serious and very painful joint disease that often results in crippling disabilities. Can strike anyone at any age.

Gout. Joint pain caused by a build-up in the body of uric acid (mostly found in meats).

Some Causes Of Arthritis
- Inadequate diet
- Little exercise
- Overweight
- General wear and tear
- Genetic factors
- Increased production of uric acid (too much meat in diet, especially organ meats)

ALZHEIMER'S DISEASE

Alzheimer's disease is a progressive, degenerative condition that attacks the brain. It results in impaired memory, decreased intellectual and emotional functioning, and ultimately complete physical breakdown.

Alzheimer's is said to affect four million American adults.

Some Causes Of Alzheimer's

- Alcohol
- Constricted arteries
- Drug reactions
- Environmental toxins
- Nutritional deficiencies
- Allergies
- Candida
- Depression
- Infections such as AIDS, meningitis, and syphilis

PNEUMONIA

Pneumonia is a severe inflammation of the lungs and is reportedly the fifth leading cause of death in the United States. It leads all other infectious diseases in mortality. This disease is especially threatening to the elderly. It is reportedly the most widespread of all fatal hospital-acquired infections.

Some Causes Of Pneumonia
- Compromised immune system
- Chronic lung diseases
- Debilitating illnesses
- Bacteria
- Fungi
- Viruses

Proper diet and nutritional supplementation can boost the immune system to combat this occurrence in the body.

OTHER RESPIRATORY CONDITIONS

Hay Fever
Hay fever is an allergic condition that is commonly associated with pollen. It affects one out of every ten Americans.

Some Things That Can Trigger This Condition In The Body
- Dog and cat hair
- Certain foods
- Dust

- Mold
- Certain medications
- Some perfumes

Asthma
An asthma attack is a condition where the bronchial passages are narrowed. This is coupled with excessive mucus that results in impaired breathing and wheezing. The severity of the symptoms often accelerates rapidly. The asthma victim suffers periodic attacks of breathing difficulty. These attacks may be severe or mild.

Some Things That Can Trigger An Asthma Attack
- Feathers
- Dust
- Animal hair
- Mold
- Detergent
- Air pollution
- Smoke
- Preservatives
- Tobacco

- Hay fever (can lead to)
- Food allergies, especially to milk and dairy products

Chronic Condition Can Be Caused By
- Small growths in nose
- Injury of nasal bones
- Smoking
- Irritant fumes and smells

Emphysema
Emphysema is classified as a chronic obstructive pulmonary disease. It is characterized by a shortness of breath upon exertion. The patient cannot exhale without great effort.

This is often a self-induced ailment brought on by **SMOKING.** However, some people suffer from this disease due to a deficiency in serum protein, according to James and Phyllis Balch in their book, Prescription for Nutritional Healing.

Patient should also avoid dairy products, salt, eggs, meat, processed foods, junk foods, and white flour products, advises John A. Sherman, N. D. of Portland Oregon.

Lung Cancer
According to <u>Alternative Medicine: The Definitive Guide</u>, lung cancer is the most common form of this disease in both women and men, and is also the number one killer of both groups. The figures are reportedly rapidly rising for women.

Some Causes Of Lung Cancer
- Smoking
- Air pollution
- Exposure to toxic industrial materials such as asbestos, coal tars, and chemical pollutants

CONSTIPATION

Constipation is the failure of the bowels to excrete fecal matter at proper intervals. This is due to sluggish action of the bowels. Constipation can be a serious condition that can result in many problems.

Proper elimination is necessary to avoid a buildup of toxins and poisons in the body that could lead to many life-threatening diseases.

Some Causes Of Constipation

- Improper diet
- Lack of fiber in the diet
- Food allergies
- Lack of exercise
- Poor posture
- Emotional instability
- Misuse of laxatives

According to Alternative Medicine: The Definitive Guide, side-effects from hundreds of common medications, including some antibiotics, antacids, muscle relaxants, and diuretics may contribute to constipation.

Alternative medicine offers a variety of approaches to help cleanse the colon and return it to a natural state of health. However, do not begin an herbal cleanse without first consulting a health care professional. For information on herbal cleanses, send a self-addressed, stamped envelope to: Herbs

For Life, 1346 W. 155th Street, Gardena, CA 90247.

GASTROINTESTINAL DISORDERS

Colitis And Crohn's Disease
These disorders involve inflammation and possible ulceration of the digestive tract. **Colitis** is confined to the colon; **Chron's Disease,** the small intestine, and somtimes the mouth, esophagus, and stomach.

Causes Of These Disorders
- Food allergies
- Autoimmune disorders

Irritable Bowel Syndrome
Irritable bowel syndrome is a condition that causes the large intestine (colon) to operate abnormally.

Some Causes Of This Disorder
- Food allergies
- Excess dietary fats
- Stress

Ulcers

An ulcer is an open sore. Ulcers occur along the gastrointestinal tract—especially in the stomach, small intestines, and colon.

Some Possible Causes of Ulcers

- Overuse of aspirin
- Other anti-inflammatory medications
- Food allergies and nutritional problems may also be responsible, according to Dr. James Braly, Medical Director of Immuno Labs, Inc., in Ft. Lauderdale, FL.

Diverticulosis And Diverticulitis

Diverticulosis is a condition that causes the walls of the intestines to balloon out forming pouches. **Diverticulitis** is an inflammation of these pouches which occurs when undigested food particles lodge in these pouches causing irritation and inflammation.

Diverticulosis and Diverticulitis are much easier to prevent than to treat. I, and many other natural health professionals, believe that these conditions are solely the result of the standard American diet that is so deficient in life-preserving properties.

Diarrhea

Diarrhea, watery, loose bowel movements, is a common symptom of many disorders. If not resolved in a few days, medical attention should be sought.

According to Dr. Donovan, chronic diarrhea may be due to food allergies.

If you will notice, diet plays a role in the formation of all of the above conditions in the body.

There are herbal programs that have been historically known to help alleviate, and sometimes even eradicate, the symptoms of these conditions from the body. To obtain programs for specific conditions, please send a self-addressed, stamped envelope to:

Herbs For Life
1346 W. 155th Street
Gardena, CA 90247

OTHER CONDITIONS/BAD HABITS

Obesity.

Obesity has been linked to many health problems including heart disease, diabetes, high blood pressure, gall-bladder disease, respiratory conditions, breast and other forms of cancer in women, and cancer of the colon and rectum. This condition has been shortening the life span of many for years.

According to Barbara M. Dixon, L.D.N, R.D. in her book, Good Health for African Americans, obesity can alter the body's hormones, contributing to low sperm count and impotency in men, and reproductive problems in women that may prove to be hazardous to both mothers and babies during pregnancy and childbirth.

Weight loss is a national obsession in America, with millions of men, women, and children being caught up in the frenzy of trying to loose the bulge. Diet after diet has come and gone with little or no success. The best-planned diets seem to work for only a little while, with most people losing then gaining it all beck within a year's time.

According to Majid Ali, M.D., Alternative Medicine: The Definitive Guide, Dieting can lead to emaciation of muscle cells. It can also bloat fat cells, cause the body to be fatigued, and cause an accumulation of toxic fats in tissues. The faster the weight loss, the greater the risk of heart complications.

Obesity is considered one of America's modern day plagues.

The number of overweight people in this country is constantly on the rise, and the problem will continue to get worse until the American citizens learn the truth about eating properly and take responsibility for their own bodies.

Some Causes of Obesity
- Overeating
- One's culture
- Environment
- Exercise habits

- Eating styles
- One's genetic makeup
- Biochemical individuality
- Physiological "set point"
- Glandular problems (small percentage)

(The "set point" theory states that one's size and body fat are determined by genetics, eating patterns and calorie intake at certain key times in life such as early adolescence. Research shows that the set point can be reset by gradually reducing calories and increasing physical activity.)

It is this author's opinion that overeating and wrong food combining are two of the major causes of obesity. The American diet is grossly unhealthy, consisting of damaging foods as well as non-food items, for it does not satisfy our nutritional needs. When we eat devitalized foods, void of vitamins and minerals, our body tells us that it is still in need of sustenance, so we continue to eat, trying to satisfy our hunger. Because of the inadequate food of which the American diet is comprised, we have destroyed our bodies' natural ability to warn us when to stop eating which often results in overeating that leads to an obese body. On the other hand, when we consume nutritious food, our body recognizes when it has enough and warns us to stop eating.

When we completely understand how harmful being overweight is, and how it can predispose us to detrimental illnesses, we will realize how important it is to control our eating habits.

Below are some **unhealthy habits** you might address if you are overweight:

- Eating when you are bored, anxious, or frustrated
- Substituting food for other desires, such as affection or love
- Overeating
- Eating in front of the TV
- Eating too fast
- Improper chewing of food
- Drinking with meals

- Binging after starving one's self trying to lose weight
- Eating standing up or lying down
- Going to bed too soon after eating
- Improper food combining (meat and potatoes)

Some Foods To Avoid
(According to Louise Tenney in her book, Modern Day Plagues, the following foods inhibit the action of the pituitary gland and hinder the hormones ability to metabolize fats. They also stay in the intestinal tract too long and promote weight gain.)

Caffeine drinks (coffee, cola, tea, etc.)
White flour and bakery products
Creamed vegetables
Candy
Sweet wines
Waffles and pancakes
Pasta
Jams and Jellies
White sugar products
Ice cream

Beer   Potato chips
Sweetened canned fruit
Processed cereal

Some Foods To Enjoy

Herbs
Whole grain cereals
Brown rice
Fresh (or lightly steamed) fruits and
    vegetables
Fresh fruit and vegetable juices
Sprouts

Foods That Heal.

(Fruits are the cleansers of the body, and
vegetables are the builders. Lightly steamed
vegetables provide minerals.)

Carrots   Tomatoes
Celery   Apples
Broccoli   Cantaloupe
Beets   Berries
Lemon Water (Cleanse Liver) Melons

Plums   Asparagus   Whole grains
Chives   Seaweed
Cabbage (red, savoy)

Alcohol Consumption.
    "It is good neither to eat flesh, nor to drink wine, nor any thing whereby thy brother stumbleth, or is offended, or is made weak." Romans 14:21.
    "Wine is a mocker, strong drink is raging: and whosoever is deceived thereby is not wise." Proverbs 20:1.
    "Be not among winebibbers; among riotous eaters of flesh: For the drunkard and the glutton shall come to poverty; and drowsiness shall clothe a man with rags". Proverbs 23:20-21.
    "Who hath redness of eyes... They that tarry long at the wine; they that go to seek mixed wine." Proverbs 23:29-30.
    "At the last it biteth like a serpent, and stingeth like an adder. Thine eyes shall behold strange women, and thine heart shall utter perverse things." Proverbs 23: 32-33.

Alcohol consumption makes man quite foolish. The drunkard ends up doing things he/she would not normally do. He/she does things he/she can't even remember. The alcoholic says ungodly things—to anybody. In other words, the drunkard acts the fool and swears he/she is "just fine," just as lucid, mentally sound, and alert as anybody else. And he/she truly believes this, because the alcohol will have taken control of the senses.

This author does not consider this killer of approximately 100,000 Americans annually a disease, but rather weak will-power—a bad habit that, for some, got out of control.

This condition is totally preventable.

Over consumption of alcohol might begin with what is termed as "social drinking" and the misconception that drinking is synonymous with having a "good time."

Peer pressure is also a major problem, because a surprising number of teenagers tend to not think for themselves, but allow others to think for them, often leading them into traps that they would not fall prey to ordinarily. Even children in elementary school are feeling the strain. For the younger generation, alcohol combined with a diet saturated with sugar and starch and the pressure to have a "good time," sets the stage for a long-term addiction.

Dr. Cass Ingram, in his book, Eat Right To Live Long, states that nearly all ingested alcohol gets into the system after one or two hours. Once in the blood, most of the alcohol is absorbed by the liver, which attempts to break it down. The rest is excreted by the lungs (the breath), the kidneys (the urine), and through the skin. Some liver damage can occur from even as few as two or three drinks per week.

Dr. Igram also states that alcohol is directly toxic to cells and cell membranes, and that direct damage can occur to the stomach and intestinal wall as well as to the brain, spinal cord, and the pancreas. He further states that alcoholics are much more likely to develop other diseases and even suffer fatalities from heart disease and cancer, the number one and number two killers.

Alcohol abuse also promotes low-birth-weight and malformed babies, mentally impaired babies, damage to the nervous system, and violent behavior.

Alcoholism does not only kill the alcoholic but also innocent victims. According to Dr. Cass, statistics show that the major factor in fatal industrial accidents is drinking on the job; that nearly one out of every two deaths from car accidents is alcohol-related; and that a high percentage of mass transportation accidents, including airline mishaps, is related to the drinking habits of the crew.

It is my opinion that alcohol is truly a poison and should be strictly avoided. It creates its own killer disease in the body: **cirrhosis of the liver.** And...socially, few people are looked down upon more than the drunkard. Not only does he/she act abnormally, but the drunkard smells. That smell permeates the entire body—not just one's breath—rendering the person most offensive. The sad thing is that the alcoholic is usually the last, if ever, to recognize that he/she has a problem and is, therefore, reluctant to try to help him/herself.

Alternative approaches are in place to help assist the alcoholic with this problem.

Illegal Drug Abuse.
It never ceases to baffle me that so many people choose to alter their minds and create havoc in their bodies by using drugs. I simply can't conceive the depth of their ignorance. We see people all around us, walking the streets like zombies, out of their minds—their brains (the computer of all computers that God provided all of us with to use in a constructive and enhancing manner) literally fried by drugs.

This habit is demeaning, demoralizing, and, in this author's opinion, suicidal. Yet, the problem continues in our society.

I believe this, too, like alcohol, is not an illness but a self-induced problem of weakness, the lack of willpower to resist the temptation. Unless drugs are forced upon an individual against his/her will, or unless some careless, morally corrupt person gives drugs to a child who is too young to resist or know better than to take them, there is no reason a person should violate his/her most precious possession, God's temple, with such vile substances.

The argument we sometimes get from addicts is, "It's not our fault. We don't bring the drugs into our neighborhood." And I say to that, "What has that got to do with anything? Maybe you didn't bring the drugs into your neighborhood. Maybe you didn't bring the drugs into the country either. But do you have to accept everything that is offered to you? If someone handed you a bottle with the word, *POISON,* printed on it and told you to drink from it, would you?" Same difference. Or, sometimes, we hear, "I thought I could handle it." To that one, I say, "What made you think you could handle it when others could not? How did you think you were so different?" Or the most foolish of all, "Everybody is doing it." To this, I say, "You could not be so wrong. I am somebody, and I wouldn't touch the stuff."

There are many people who have better sense than to experiment with drugs. I know quite a few.

The solution to the overall problem is for people to resist the temptation no matter how appetizing and appealing the substance may be.

"Yield not to temptation..."

If the pushers did not have customers, they would soon go out of business. Simple deduction. Literally killing ones self to make someone else rich sounds rather foolish to me.

Following the crowd when you know it is going in the wrong direction takes no brains. God gave you some sense. Use it. Be your own person. Think for yourself. Be a leader rather than a follower. You might learn to like the feeling.

The drug problem is so prolific in the United States, there are probably few, if any, families that it has not touched in some way. It has certainly touched mine. No one could have been more shocked than I when I heard that some of my younger family members were caught up in this insanity. I refused to believe it. "The Dumas children know better than to mess with that poison," I said. "They were brought up right. In the church. They are all good children. They know better! Somebody is lying!" But in spite of my disbelief and rage, it was true. My family had been stricken by this madness. I was devastated, disappointed, and angry. I am still so very angry with one of the younger members of my family who lost his life because of drug involvement. I am trying to let go of that anger, but I can't seem to do so, because I know he knew better than to start such a detrimental habit that eventually led to his death.

Addictions are most damaging to the brain, the nervous and digestive systems, the pancreas and the liver. Drugs can literally destroy brain cells and weaken the hypothalamus (appetite control), creating a craving or addiction. Addictions deplete essential vitamins and minerals while giving a false sense of energy.

Drugs also weaken the immune system, leaving the body vulnerable to diseases that can kill such as cancer and heart attacks. Drug abuse is also associated with HIV infection and AIDS.

According to Barbara M. Dixon, L.D.N., R.D., in her book, <u>Good Health for African Americans</u> any kind of drug addiction (heroin, marijuana, cocaine, or crack) produces a vast range of emotional and negative mental effects on the body. These effects can range from poor concentration to acute anxiety, paranoia, mood swings, and hallucinations. The addict is also usually angered easily and sometimes experiences crying spells and slurred speech patterns.

Cocaine has been known to cause:
- Coronary artery spasms
- Heart attacks

- Violent behavior
- Respiratory problems
- Decrease in appetite
- Death

Marijuana has been known to cause:
- Increased heart rate
- Impaired functioning of brain
- Emphysema
- Bronchitis
- Cancer of the lungs

Because the drug addict's body normally craves sugar and simple carbohydrates, this person's body is usually protein deficient. Therefore, the addict's condition can only be helped when his/her nutrient deficiency has been changed through dietary habits to help prevent cravings for the drugs.

Smoking.
In my opinion, smoking is one of the nastiest, the most unnecessary, the most

detrimental, dangerous—not just to the smoker but to others as well—suicidal habits that man ever dared to embrace. Nothing is glamorous—as the tobacco industry tries to purport—about it. There is nothing smart, "cool" or fun about it. It is slow suicide. As with illegal drugs, rather than picking up on this bad habit, people should literally run from it. Anyone with a functioning brain in his/her head should know that if others are dying and suffering from painful diseases brought on by a substance, he/she should not follow the same path. Why, then, is this habit so appealing to some of America's younger generation? Someone please explain it to me, because I just do not understand.

To Our Teenagers (Our Future):

I am sure you know by now what doctors and other professionals say about smoking: it contributes to lung cancer, heart disease, and emphysema. When considering these three conditions alone, you should experience an immediate "brain alert" that lets you know this substance is **bad for your health**. In addition to eventually giving you a terminal disease, this substance makes you smell—your breath, your clothes, your body—you literally stink, and your fingers and teeth turn yellow. Smoking makes others avoid you. Smokers are rapidly becoming social outcasts. It is also expensive, and the price for this product is going up constantly. If you think it makes you look "grown-up"—it doesn't. If you have to hide to do it, do you really feel grown-up? It is a fact that nicotine is habit-forming. Smoking can eventually contribute to certain deadly diseases, it offends others, and makes you socially unacceptable. In other words, it is a stupid habit. Millions of smokers have kicked the habit. Many more are trying. If you smoke, quit. If you don't, don't start. Don't listen to the tale that "everybody else does it." They don't. And even if every-body else did, why would you want to be as stupid as everybody else? Someone **must** have some sense. Why not let it be you?

Some Hazards Of Smoking

- Each cigarette steals away approximately eight minutes of your life.
- One pack a day is equivalent to losing approximately a month of life each year.
- One cigarette can reportedly increase your heart rate twenty to twenty-five beats per minute.
- One cigarette can cause a significant increase in blood pressure.
- Cigarettes contain four thousand known toxic poisons.
- Smoking depletes vitamin C in the body.
- Cigarettes reportedly increase carbon monoxide levels in the blood.
- The circulatory system takes up to six hours to return to normal after smoking just one cigarette.
- Smoking is immunosuppressive.
- It reportedly takes three months to reverse cigarette damage to the immune system.

- Smoking is linked to lung cancer.
- Cigarette smoking is the major cause of emphysema.

FROM DATA COMPILED BY THE AMERICAN CANCER SOCIETY AND THE AMERICAN HEART ASSOCIATION

Risks
- **Shortened Life Expectancy:** Risk is proportional to number of packs smoked and length of time one has smoked. The average smoker can expect to live fewer years than a nonsmoker.
- **Heart Disease:** Smokers are twice as likely to have a heart attack as non-smokers, and are five times more likely to die of sudden death from heart attack.
- **Lung Cancer:** Cigarette smoking is responsible for 80% to 85% of all lung cancers. Lung cancer is the leading cause of cancer death among American men and women.

- **Peripheral Vascular Disease:** Because it accelerates "hardening of the arteries" and encourages platelet adhesion (stickiness), smoking can negatively affect blood circulation in the legs, which can lead to gangrene and amputation.
- **Larynx Cancer:** Smoking increases risk by about three to eighteen times that of nonsmokers.
- **Mouth Cancer:** Smokers have three to ten times as many oral cancers as nonsmokers. Pipes, cigars, and snuff are also major risk factors.
- **Cancer of Esophagus:** Cigarettes, pipes and cigars increase risk of dying from this cancer two to nine times.
- **Cancer of Bladder:** Smokers' risk is seven to ten times greater.
- **Cancer of Pancreas:** Risk of dying from this cancer is two to five times higher than for nonsmokers.
- **Chronic Bronchitis and Emphysema:** Smokers face four to 25 times greater risks of death from these diseases.

- **Stillbirth, Prematurity, Low-Birth Weight, and SIDS:** Smoking women have more stillbirths, more low-birth weight babies, more babies who are vulnerable to disease and death, and Sudden Infant Death Syndrome.

Benefits of Quitting

- **Life Expectancy:** After 10 to 15 years, ex-smokers mortality rates approach that of people who have never smoked.
- **Heart Disease:** Risk decreases sharply after one year of nonsmoking. After 10 years, risk approaches that of people who have never smoked.
- **Peripheral Vascular Disease:** Risk decreases.
- **Lung Cancer:** After 10 to 15 years, risk approaches that of people who have never smoked.
- **Larynx Cancer:** Gradual reduction in risk, normal after 10 years.
- **Mouth cancer:** Eliminating smoking and drinking lowers risk in a few years.

- **Cancer of Esophagus:** Eliminating smoking and drinking should lower risk.
- **Cancer of Bladder:** Risk decreases gradually to that of nonsmokers over seven years.
- **Cancer of Pancreas:** Should reduce risk.
- **Chronic Bronchitis and Emphysema:** Within weeks, cough disappears. Lung function may improve, and rate of deterioration may slow down.
- **Stillbirth, Prematurity, Low-Birth Weight, and SIDS:** Risk to fetus reduces if mother quits smoking before fourth month.

Smoking can also lead to malnutrition by depleting the body of essential vitamins and minerals such as calcium that may lead to osteoporosis.

Secondhand (passive) smoke inhaled by nonsmokers can also pose many health hazards. Secondhand smoke reportedly causes thousands of deaths annually and from 150 to 300 thousand cases of respiratory illness such as pneumonia, bronchitis, and asthma.

Alternatives to Kicking This Bad Habit

Just quit. It is easier for some than others. It takes strong motivation and determination, but it can be done. First, get the drug out of your head. See yourself functioning without a cigarette between your fingers. Set a date, and never smoke another cigarette from that day forward.

Replace cigarettes with something wholesome. Eat carrots, prunes, or chew on cinnamon sticks...

Cut down gradually. You can do this on your own or join a self-help group such as Smokenders.

Or...

Do as a friend of mine did: **Ask the Lord to remove the craving from you.** My friend said she did not ask Him to help her stop smoking, but left it all in His hands because she knew she did not have the willpower, and that He did not need any help in taking the addiction from her. She said she prayed one night asking Him to take the craving, and the next day, it was three o'clock in the afternoon before she thought about a cigarette. Her smokes immediately after breakfast and lunch, and in between, had been completely forgotten. She knew the Lord had indeed answered her prayer. She said she threw her cigarettes away and has not had a desire to smoke since.

"And I say unto you, Ask, and it shall be given you..." Luke 11:9.

It is this author's opinion that proper life-style management and the right diet could prevent all of the diseases/conditions we just explored. There are also herbs designed to help the alcohol abuser, drug abuser, and smoker with their bad habits.

And now, let us take a look at some foods from God's garden.

4

FOOD FROM
GOD'S GARDEN

CHAPTER FOUR
Food From
God's Garden

---

*I*think that I shall never see

A poem as lovely as a tree...
Poems are made by fools like me,
But only God can make a tree.

From Joyce Kilmer's poem, Trees."

Let us begin with trees, shall we?
"...and the leaves of the tree were
for the healing of the nations." Revela-
tions 22:2.

"...on this side and on that side, shall grow all trees for meat, whose leaf shall not fade, ...and the fruit thereof shall be for meat, and the leaf thereof for medicine." Exekiel 47:12.

What better place to start than with the forbidden fruit from the proverbial apple tree that God planted in the Garden of Eden...

"And when the woman saw that the tree was good for food, and that it was pleasant to the eyes, and a tree to be desired to make one wise, she took of the fruit thereof and did eat, and gave also unto her husband with her; and he did eat." Genesis 3:6.

We all know the story. And we know that Eve should not have gotten that apple and offered it to her husband. But, then, did her husband have to take it and eat of it? The man could have refused. But he did not. Adam ate. They sinned together. They ate the forbidden fruit. But in spite of Eve's disobedience, maybe she should be given a little credit for being wise enough to pluck a fruit that was most beneficial to her and her husband's bodies. According to Barbara Flot, N. D.,C.N.H.P, Los Angeles, "The apple feeds every system in the body."

THE APPLE TREE

Most of us have heard the old adages: "An apple a day keeps the doctor away," and "To eat an apple before going to bed, will make the doctor beg his bread." These sayings just might be truer than we think—especially if the doctor happens to be a gastroenterologist, cardiologist, or oncologist.

The apple is reportedly good for both diarrhea and constipation and may help prevent heart disease, cancer and some types of stroke—some of America's top killers.

- **Diarrhea** - adds bulk to stool, helping to relieve diarrhea and provides protective coating for irritated intestinal lining.
- **Constipation** - Adds bulk to stool that stimulates normal bowel contractions.

- **Heart Disease and stroke** - Apple helps reduce blood cholesterol, a key factor for heart disease and some types of stroke.
- **Cancer** - According to a study of the National Cancer Institute, pectin binds certain cancer-causing compounds in the colon, speeding their elimination from the body.
- **Diabetes**- Studies show that apple pectin helps control blood sugar levels.
- **Lead Poisoning** - Studies show that apple pectin helps eliminate lead, mercury, and other toxic heavy metals from body.
- **Wound Infection** - Apple leaves contain an antibiotic that aids in the healing of infections. Leaves can be wrapped around or pressed into the wound as first aid.

Caution: Eat the apple, but stay away from the seeds. They contain a high level of **cyanide.**

THE BLACK COHOSH TREE

It appears the Indians were right about this herb. They boiled black cohosh roots in water then drank the tea for fatigue, sore throat, arthritis, and rattle-snake bite—hence another popular name for this herb, "snakeroot." This herb was primarily used by Indian women for gynecological problems and childbirth.

Other uses

Astringent
Bee stings
Childbirth
Convulsions
Diuretic
Epilepsy
Hormone balancer
Hot flashes
Hysteria
Lumbago
Menopause
Menstrual problems
Nervousness
Neuralgia
Paralysis
Poison antidote
Prostate cancer
Spasms
St. Vitus Dance
Syphilis
Tuberculosis
Typhoid fever
Whooping cough
Worms

Caution: Estrogenic herbs must be used carefully. Women who have been advised not to take "the pill" should not take black cohosh. An overdose of this herb could cause a few side-effects such as dizziness, or headache. **Pregnant women** and **people with risk of cancer** should not take black cohosh.

THE BLACK WALNUT TREE

Black walnut oxygenates the blood to kill parasites. It is also used to help balance sugar levels and burn up excessive toxins and fatty materials in the body. The brown stain found in the green husk contains organic iodine which has antiseptic and healing properties.

This herb can be used for restoring tooth enamel and contains constituents which have been found to be an antidote for electrical shock. It can be used for poison oak, ringworm and skin problems. It also aids in bowel cleansing, and thyroid problems.

Other uses

Abscesses	Lupus
Acne	Mouth sores
Antiseptic, external	Piles, bleeding
Boils	Poison Ivy
Cancer	Tonsillitis
Colitis	Tuberculosis
Diphtheria	Tumors
Fevers	Ulcers, internal
Goiter	Uterus, prolapsed
Gum disease	Varicose veins
Infections (internal)	Worms
Lactation, stops	Wounds
Liver problems	

THE CASCARA SAGRADA TREE

Cascara sagrada was called the "wonder of the new world." The Spanish recognized this herb as a relative of buckthorn, the powerful laxative herb used in Europe since ancient times. However, cascara sagrada was much gentler. In Spanish, cascara sagrada means "sacred bark."

For a long time, cascara sagrada remained a folk remedy known as "chitten bark," a polite variant of the Gold Rush '49er' name, 'sh—tin' bark. The purgative power of this herb has earned it a reputation as the world's most widely used laxative. It is the main ingredient in some over-the-counter laxatives.

Some uses

Bowels (toxic)	High blood
Constipation	Indigestion
Colitis	Insomnia
Croup	Intestines
Digestion	Liver disorders
Gallbladder (sluggish)	Nerves
Gallstones	Parasites
Gout	Spleen
Hemorrhoids	Worms

Caution: No laxative should be used constantly. Cascara sagrada should be used in medicinal amounts only. This herb has been known to regulate the bowels.

Avoid this herb if you are pregnant, have ulcers, colitis, hemorrhoids, or gastrointestinal conditions.

THE CINNAMON TREE

Cinnamon is one of the world's oldest healers. The Biblical Hebrews, Greeks, and Romans used it as a spice, perfume, and treatment for indigestion. In the 12th century, German herbalist Hildegard recommended it for sinuses and to treat colds, flu, cancer, and "inner decay and slime."

Other Uses

Abdominal spasms
Cholera
Colic (infant)
Diarrhea
Digestive aid
Flatulence
Indigestion
Infection (prevent)
Menstruation (excess)
Nausea/vomiting
Stomach cramps

Cinnamon is used as a flavoring agent for bitter-tasting healing preparations. Some say it stimulates uterine contractions; others say it calms the uterus.

Caution: Pregnant women should limit their use to culinary amounts. Other women might try cinnamon to bring on menstruation or after delivery. The powdered form of cinnamon (culinary amounts) are nontoxic. However **cinnamon oil** is just the opposite. **Do not ingest cinnamon oil.**

THE JUNIPER TREE

In the 17th century, juniper was used as a diuretic to increase urine production. Noted English herbalists reportedly prescribed the herb for dropsy (congestive heart failure), cough, shortness of breath, consumption (tuberculosis), to provoke terms (menstruation), and give safe and speedy delivery to women with child.

Studies suggest that juniper stimulates the uterine contractions. Pregnant women should not use it, except at term when it might help stimulate labor.

It may help relieve bloated feeling caused by premenstrual fluid retention; PMS sufferers might try juniper during the uncomfortable days just before their periods.

Some Uses

Adrenal problems	Gas
Arthritis	Gout
Bladder problems	Gonorrhea
Bleeding	Infections
Colds/coughs	Insect bites
Colic	Piles
Congestive heart failure	Snakebite
Contagious diseases	Tuberculosis
Convulsions	Typhoid fever
Cramps	Uric acid build up
Cystitis	Urinary disorders
Diabetes	Water retention
Dysentery	Worms

Caution: Juniper should not be given to children under two years of age. For older

children and people over 65, start with low
strength preparations and increase if necessary. This herb should not be used by
anyone with kidney problems. Do not take
if taking diuretics. Take only as directed,
and never longer than six weeks at a time.

THE PAPAYA TREE

Papaya contains digestive enzymes
that are the key to its healing value as a
digestive aid. The most important digestive
enzyme in papaya is papain that is similar to
the human digestive enzyme, pepsin, which
helps break down protein. (Digestive
enzymes are needed to help with the
digestion of certain foods. This is especially
true when one eats cooked foods.)

The Indians used the milky fluid
called latex from the mature, but un-ripe
papaya to treat psoriasis, ringworm,
wounds, and infections. Caribbean Indian
women ate unripe papaya to trigger labor.
Filipinos used a root decoction to treat
hemorrhoids.

Some Uses

Belching
Colon conditions
Constipation
Digestive aid
Diverticulitis

Diarrhea, chronic
Gas
Intestinal tract
Stomach
   problems
Worms

Caution: Pregnant women should eat this fruit in moderation, as it could induce labor or possibly trigger a miscarriage.

THE PAU D'ARCO TREE

Pau D'Arco has beneficial effects on the whole body, increases resistance to disease, and builds the immune system. It also kills viruses, is an antibacterial agent, aids in smoker's cough, is very effective against all types of cancers, helps insomnia and anxiety. This herb can be used to build blood, aid in digestion, and help with circulation.

Other Uses

Age spots	Lupus
AIDS	Nephritis
Arteriosclerosis	Pain (relieves)
Asthma	Parasites
Bronchitis	Parkinson's disease
Colitis	Polyps
Cystitis	Prostatitis
Diabetes	Psoriasis
Eczema	Respiratory problems
Gastritis	Rheumatism
Gonorrhea	Ringworm
Hemorrhages	Spleen infections
Herpes	Syphilis
Intestines	Ulcers
Leukemia	Varicose veins
Liver Ailments	Venereal Disease

THE SLIPPERY ELM TREE

The slippery elm tree is called "The tree that shades and soothes." It was historically used to treat sore throat, cough colds, inflamed nipples, and gastrointestinal ailments. It was also used to feed infants and hospital patients. Slippery elm was also used to treat syphilis, gonorrhea, and hemorrhoids. When applied to wounds, it dries to form an herbal bandage. Slippery elm has a beneficial effect on the whole body. It absorbs noxious gases, neutralizes stomach acidity; strengthens, heals, and soothes inflamed or irritated areas.

Some Uses

Appendicitis	Herpes
Asthma	Inflammations
Bladder problems	Lung problems
Boils	Phlegm
Bronchitis	Pneumonia
Burns	Stomach problems
Cancer	Syphilis
Colitis	Tuberculosis
Colon problems	Tumors
Constipation	Ulcers
Croup	Worms
Diaper rash	Whooping cough

Digestive problems   Hemorrhoids
Diarrhea   Gastrointestinal
Female problems   problems

THE MELALEUCA TREE
(Tea Tree Oil)

The oil from the melaleuca tree of Australia (tea tree oil) has been known for its healing properties for over two centuries. Tea tree oil contains forty-eight natural organic substances that work together to produce its healing powers. Tea tree oil has over 100 uses.

Some Uses

Acne   Itchy scalp
Antiseptic   Leg ulcers
Aromatherapy   Minor cuts & abrasions
Athletes foot   Muscle aches
Baby care   Nappy rash
Bath soak   Nail soak
Bedsores   Nasal congestion
Blisters   Ovarian cysts

Bruises
Congestion
Callouses
Canker sores
Chapped lips
Cleansing Hair
Cold sores
Cradle cap
Dandruff
Dental abscesses
Dermatitis
Diaper cleanser
Diffuser
Disinfectant
Dry hair
Ear infections
Ear mites
Eczema
Emphysema
Fleas
Fungus
Gingivitis
Head lice
Herpes
Hives

Parasites
Plantar Wart
Plaque
Poison Ivy & Oak
Psoriasis
Rashes
Ringworm
Sandfleas
Sciatica
Shingles
Sinusitis
Skin allergies
Skin rashes
Sore & bleeding gums
Sore throat
Sprains
Styes
Sunburn
Thrush
Ticks & Leeches
Toothache
Vaginal cleansing
Vaporizer
Warts
Yeast infection

THE WHITE OAK TREE

White oak contains properties for clotting, shrinking and disinfecting. It is used on sores and wounds to prevent infections. It is also healing for herpes, thrush, varicose veins and candidiasis.

Some Ailments/Uses

Bites (insect and snake)
Bladder problems
Bleeding (internal and
  external)
Blood Urine
Cancer
Dental problems
Diarrhea
Fever
Fever blisters
Gangrene
Glandular swellings
Goiter
Hemorrhoids
Indigestion

Mouth Sores
Nausea
Skin irritations
Sore gums
Strep throat
Tonsillitis
Ulcers
Uterus (prolapsed)
Vaginitis
Varicose veins
Venereal diseases
Vomiting
Worms
Wounds
  (external)

Kidney problems   Menstrual
Liver problems   problems

THE WHITE WILLOW TREE

White willow grew on the banks of the Nile, and the ancient Egyptians considered it a symbol of joy. The Hebrews adopted it, and in Leviticus (23:40) God commanded them to celebrate the autumn harvest festival by setting up temporary shelters covered with willow boughs:

"And ye shall take you on the first day the boughs of goodly trees, branches of palm trees, and the boughs of thick trees, and willows of the brook; and ye shall rejoice before the Lord your God seven days."

But the willow tree became a symbol of sorrow in Psalms 137:1-2.

"By the rivers of Babylon, there we sat down, yea, we wept, when we remembered Zion. We hanged our harps upon the willows in the midst thereof."

Since that time, the graceful tree has been known as the weeping willow.

Chinese physicians have used white willow bark to relieve pain since 500 B.C. Studies suggest that white willow may reduce blood sugar, prevent heart attacks and strokes. Other studies suggest that white willow may help reduce deaths from four digestive tract cancers: tumors of the esophagus, stomach, colon and rectum, and that it may prevent or reduce migraines.

Other Uses

Bleeding	Menstrual cramps
Chills	Night sweats
Fever	Pain
Gout	Sex depressant
Headache	Sore muscles
Infections	Worms
Impotence	Wounds

Caution: Pregnant women, nursing mothers and people who have ulcers or gastritis should not take this herb. White Willow bark should not be given to children under the age of two or to those under sixteen with a cold, flu, or chicken pox.

OTHER HERBS/FOODS FROM GOD'S GARDEN

The following herbs have historical uses of benefiting the body in various ways. Listed are some uses of these herbs. (Use only with the advice of a health care practitioner.)

ALFALFA

Acid stomach	Diuretic
Allergies	Fatigue
Anemia	Fever
Appendicitis	Gout
Appetite stimulant	Heart disease
Arthritis	Hemorrhages
Bad breath	High blood
Cancer	Hypoglycemia
Cramps	Jaundice

| Diabetes | Kidney (cleanser) |
| Digestion | Stroke |

Alfalfa cleans deep in the cells; helps in chemical imbalance; binds cholesterol, radioactive deposits and toxins in the system for elimination. Eight digestive enzymes in alfalfa provide better digestion and assimilation. It strengthens the nervous system, rebuilds decayed teeth, and benefits pituitary gland.

ALOE VERA

Bites	Skin problems
Burns	Sores
Colon problems	Stomach problems
Digestion	Sunburn
Deodorant	Tapeworms
Leg ulcers	Tuberculosis
Liver problems	Tumors
Menopause	Ulcers
Obesity	Wrinkling of skin
Poison Ivy & Oak	Vaginitis
Ringworm	Worms

Scalds   Wounds
Scar Tissue

Aloe Vera prevents the spread of infection; softens skin; cleans, heals, soothes and relieves pain on contact; stimulates colon, and eliminates toxins; relieves itching in shingles and chicken pox.

BEE POLLEN

Allergies   Hay fever
Appetite stimulant   Hypoglycemia
Asthma   Immune system
Blood pressure (lowers)   Longevity
Depression   Multiple sclerosis
Endurance   Radiation
Energy   Vitality

Bee pollen stimulates the glands to promote a feeling of rejuvenation. It reportedly slows down the aging process, and helps the hormonal system. It is a complete blood building food.

BILBERRY

Eye health (overall)	Immune system
Blood vessels	Varicose veins
Kidney problems	

Bilberry is beneficial for overall eye health and as a nutritive herb. Some have benefited within a few months for night blindness when using this herb.

Personal testimony. *(I began seeing flashes and spots before my eyes, and was told by a doctor at a well-known hospital in Los Angeles, "You're just getting old. These things happen." I did not need a second opinion to know that was a misdiagnosis and that there was something wrong with my eyes. I began using Bilberry and later had my eyes examined by an iridologist. He told me that cataracts were forming and for me to continue taking the Bilberry. After using this herb daily for approximately two years, I noticed that I could not see clearly out of my eyeglasses anymore. Upon having my eyes examined, the optometrist discovered that my lenses were too strong, that I needed less strength instead of more. He could not believe his finding. He literally followed me out the door, examining* *my eyes one last time. "I just want to be sure I'm not making a mistake," he said.*

BLESSED THISTLE

Birth control   Hormone balancer
Cancer   Lactation
Cramps   Menstrual problems
Constipation   Senility
Fevers   Worms

Blessed thistle increases mother's milk. It is helpful for young girls in puberty; takes oxygen to brain.

BONESET

Bronchitis   Measles
Catarrh   Mumps
Chills   Rheumatism (muscular)
Colds /flu   Scarlet fever
Fever & prevent   Sore throat
Jaundice   Typhoid fever
Liver disorders   Worms
Malaria   Yellow fever

Boneset is considered the best remedy for cold and flu symptoms. It cleans the stomach, liver and intestines of toxins and eliminates them from the body.

BUCHU

Bed-wetting
Bladder (weak)
Blood pressure (high)
Diabetes (first stages)
Dropsy
Gallstones
Glands
Gravel (stones)
Indigestion
Kidney problems
Liver problems
Nephritis
PMS
Rheumatism
Spleen
Urinary tract
Vaginal problems
Venereal disease
Water retention
Yeast infection

Buchu is considered one of the best herbs for the entire urinary tract; great for painful urination and bladder inflammations. It absorbs excess uric acid, thus reducing bladder irritations. It soothes the enlargement of the prostate gland and irritation of the urethral membrane.

BURDOCK

Abscesses (internal)
Acne
Allergies
Arthritis
Bladder infections
Blood poisoning
Boils
Bronchitis
Burns
Bursitis
Cancer
Canker sores
Carbuncles
Chicken Pox
Constipation
Cystitis
Degenerative conditions
Fevers
Fluid retention
Gall bladder
Hair growth
Herpes
Hypoglycemia
Infection
Inflammation
Kidney problems
Leprosy
Liver problems
Lymphatic system
Measles
Nervous disorders
Obesity
Pimples
Poisons
Psoriasis
Rheumatism
Sciatica
Skin problems
Sore throat
Stomach
Syphilis
Tonsillitis
Tumors
Uterus
   (prolapsed)

Burdock is considered one of the best blood purifiers to eliminate uric acid and excess waste materials. It soothes the hypothalamus, aids the pituitary gland to help adjust hormone balance, relieves congestion of lymphatic system, helps break down calcification in joints. Burdock is an herb to use during pregnancy. It is a strong liver purifier.

BUTCHER'S BROOM

Aneurysm
Arteriosclerosis
Blood clots
   prevent
Brain circulation
Bruises
Dropsy
Edema
Gravel
Headaches
Heavy legs
Hemorrhoids
Inflammation
Jaundice
Leg cramps
Menstrual
Phlebitis
Prostate (tumors)
Stroke
   (prevention)
Surgery (prep)
Thrombosis
Urination (scanty)
Varicose veins

Butcher's broom is effective in improving circulation to prevent post-operative thrombosis. It prevents clotting of the blood by producing a diuretic effect, strengthens the blood vessels, is an herbal food to help keep the veins clean and healthy.

CAPSICUM (Cheyenne Pepper)

Appetite stimulant
Arteriosclerosis
Arthritis
Asthma
Backache
Bleeding (ext. & int.)
Blood pressure
Bronchitis
Bruises
Burns
Chills
Circulatory disorders
Coughs/colds
Lock jaw
Lungs (fluid in)
Male tonic
Mucus
Nosebleeds
Pain (chronic)
Palsy
Paralysis
Perspiration (to
  increase)
Pyorrhea
Rheumatism
Senility
Shingles

Congestion	Shock
Contagious diseases	Sinus problems
Convulsions	Skin problems
Cramps	Sore throat
Cuts	Spasms
Digestive disorders	Sprains
Eyes	Strokes
Hangover	Surgery (prep)
Hay Fever	Tumors
Headaches	Ulcers
Heart (even during attack)	Varicose vein
Hemorrhage	Worms

Capsicum is known for its ability to ease pain, relieve headaches, reduce the risk of heart disease, stop a heart attack in progress, and cut cholesterol. Capsicum is a first-aid remedy for most conditions; stops bleeding. It is a powerful stimulant. It has the ability to rebuild tissue in the stomach and heal stomach and intestinal ulcers. It is known as the purest and best stimulant in the herb kingdom. It helps to increase the effectiveness of other herbs.

CATNIP

Bronchitis (chronic)	Gas
Circulation (improves)	Hiccups
Colds/flu	Infertility
Colic	Insanity
Convulsions	Lung congestion
Cramps (menstrual)	Miscarriage
Diarrhea	(prevention)
Digestion	Morning sickness
Diseases (childhood)	Shock
Drug withdrawal	Worms

Catnip is known as nature's "Alka-seltzer." It also has a sedative effect on the nervous system and is useful in many ailments. It will work quickly to overcome convulsions in children. When used as a warm enema, it will cleanse the colon and reduce spasms. It helps to expel excess mucus from the body. Catnip is good for restlessness and colic for small children. Reportedly, putting several drops on the back of the tongue will reduce the craving for cigarettes.

CHAMOMILE

Air pollution	Gallstones
Appetite Stimulant	Gas
Asthma (steam inhalant)	Hysteria
Bladder	Insomnia
Bronchitis	Jaundice
Childhood diseases	Kidneys
Constipation	Measles
Colds, Coughs	Nervousness
Cramps (menstrual)	Pain
Cramps (stomach)	Spasms
Diarrhea	Stomach upset
Drug withdrawal	Teething
Earache (compress)	Tumors
Eye (sore)	Typhoid
Fevers	Peptic ulcers

Camomile is one of the best herbs to keep handy for emergencies as a tea for the nerves and menstrual cramps; for small babies and children for colds, stomach trouble, colitis, and externally for eczema and inflammation. It is a soothing sedative with no side effects. It is soothing for an upset stomach in babies, and also helps to promote natural sleep.

CHICKWEED

Appetite, decrease
Arteriosclerosis
Asthma
Bleeding
Blood purifier
Bronchitis
Burns
Cancer
Colitis
Constipation
Convulsions
Cramps

Eye infections
Gas
Hemorrhoids
Lung congestion
Mucus
Obesity, cuts fat
Skin diseases
Testes (swollen)
Tissues,
   inflamed
Tumors (fatty)
Water retention

Chickweed helps with youthful appearance and mental attitude as it feeds the pineal and pituitary glands. It will help dissolve the plaque out of the blood vessels and fatty substances in the system, has antiseptic properties when exposed to the blood, and has been called an effective anti-cancer agent. Chickweed is mild and has been used as a food as well as medicine.

COMFREY

Allergies
Anemia
Asthma
Bladder problems
Bleeding
Blood Cleanser
Boils
Broken bones/sprains
Bruises
Burns
Bursitis
Cancer
Colds, coughs
Colitis
Cramps
Diarrhea
Digestion
Emphysema
Eczema

Fatigue
Fractures
Gangrene
Gum disease
Infections
Insect bites
Kidney stones
Leg cramps
Lungs
Pain
Pleurisy
Pneumonia
Respiratory
Skin problems
Sores
Stomach trouble
Swelling
Tonic (overall)
Tuberculosis

Comfrey is one of the most valuable herbs known to botanical medicine. It has been used for centuries with success as a wound-healer and bone knitter. It feeds the pituitary with its natural hormone and helps strengthen the body skeleton. It helps promote strong bones and healthy skin. It is an overall tonic and is one of the finest healers for the respiratory system. It can be used both internally and externally for healing of fractures, wounds, sores and ulcers.

CORNSILK

Arteriosclerosis	Heart trouble
Bed-wetting	High blood
Bladder problems	Kidney problems
Cholesterol	Obesity
Cystitis	Painful urination
Edema	Prostate
Gonorrhea	Urinary problems

Cornsilk is used primarily for bladder complaints.

CRANBERRY

Bladder	Kidneys
Incontinence	Urinary tract infections

Cranberry prevents bladder problems and soothes irritated membranes.

DAMIANA

Bladder	Hormone balancer
Brain tonic	Hot flashes
Energy	Menopause
Emphysema	Nervousness
Estrogen (low)	PMS
Female problems	Prostate
Frigidity	Sexual stimulant

Damiana has been recommended for increasing sperm count in the male and strengthening the egg in the female. It also helps balance the hormones in women. It is reportedly one of the safest and most popular herbs for restoring natural sexual capacities and functions.

DANDELION

Age spots
Appetite stimulant
Blisters, external
Blood cleanser
Blood purifier
Constipation
Corns
Cramps
Dermatitis
Digestive disorders
Eczema
Endurance
Female organs

Fever
Gall bladder
Gas
Hypoglycemia
Jaundice
Liver disorders
Pancreas
Psoriasis
Scurvy
Stamina
Ulcers
Warts

Dandelion is considered a nutritive herb with medicinal benefits. It has the ability to clear obstructions and stimulate the liver to detoxify poisons. It restores the gastric balance in patients who have suffered from severe vomiting. Dandelion is considered a valuable survival food. A diet of this herb also improves the enamel of the teeth.

DONG QUAI

Abdominal pain	Female glands
Anemia	Headaches, migraine
Angina	Hot flashes
Bleeding, internal	Hypertension
Blood disorders	Hypoglycemia
Brain nourisher	Lumbago
Bruises	Menopause
Chills	Muscle spasms
Circulation	Nervousness
Constipation	Tonic
Cramps (menstrual)	Vaginal dryness

Dong Quai is considered the queen of all female herbs. It promotes the growth of the womb, and is reportedly effective against almost every complaint of the female system. It is a useful herb for the mother-to-be. Men use this herb for migraines.

ECHINACEA

Antiseptic	Bladder infections
Bites/stings	Blood purifier

Blood Diseases	Laryngitis
Cancer	Lymphatic infections
Congestion	Sore throat
Emphysema	Syphilis
Fever	Tongue & mouth
Gangrene	infections
Glands	Tetanus
Gums (sore)	Tooth ache
Hemorrhoids	Typhoid fever
Immune (stimulant)	Tonsillitis
Indigestion	Tuberculosis
Infections	Tumors

Echinacea stimulates the immune response, increasing the body's ability to resist infections; purifies the blood; cleans the system.

EYEBRIGHT

Black eye (compress)	Eye (strengthens)
Cataracts	Glaucoma
Catarrh	Hay fever
Congestion	Liver stimulant
Conjunctivitis	Memory

Earache	Middle ear problems
Eye disorders	Sinus congestion
	Styes (dissolves)

Eyebright aids in stimulating the liver to clean the blood and relieve the conditions that affect the clarity of vision and thought. It will strengthen all parts of the eye and provide an elasticity to the nerves and optic devices responsible for sight.

FENNEL

Appetite depressant	Female problems
Bed-wetting	Gas (expels)
Colic	Gout
Constipation	Indigestion
Convulsions	Intestinal
Coughs	Spasms
Digestive aid	Pin worms

Fennel helps move waste material out of the body. It is also a sedative for children, and purifies the blood.

FENUGREEK

Abscess	Inflammation
Allergies	Lactation
Bad breath	Lung infections
Blood poisoning	Mucus (dissolves)
Boils	Sore throat
Bowel lubricant	Stomach irritation
Bronchial catarrh	Ulcers
Carbuncles	Vagina
Coughs	Water retention
Fevers	Wounds (poultice)

Fenugreek has the ability to soften and dissolve hardened masses of accumulated mucus, helps expel toxic waste through the lymphatic system, has antiseptic properties, and is nourishing for mother's milk.

FEVERFEW

Allergies	Colds/flu
Asthma	Fever
Chills	Hay fever

Dizziness   Migraine headaches
Hot flashes   Nervous hysteria
Insect bites   Sinus headaches
Lungs   Tinnitus

Feverfew is a natural relief for migraine headaches, and is used to provide circulation to the brain and head area.

FLAXSEED OIL

Body lubricant   Jaundice
Bronchitis   Liver complaints
Catarrhal conditions   Lung problems
Colds   Pleurisy
Constipation   Pneumonia
Gallstones   Rheumatism
Heart (strengthener)   Worms

Flaxseed oil is known as "the body's lubricant." It heals the body as it nourishes, is soothing to the throat, entire stomach and intestinal linings, and is a natural laxative. It has been used for weak babies, enriching the blood and strengthening the nerves.

GARLIC

Acne	Heart disease
Allergies	High blood pressure
Antibiotic (natural)	Hypoglycemia
Anti-fungus	Infectious diseases
Anti-viral	Insomnia
Blood Poisoning	Intestinal infections
Cancer immunity	Mucus
Colds/flu	Parasites/worms
Digestion	Pneumonia
Diverticulitis	Respiratory congestion
Ear infections	Sinus problems
Emphysema	Toxic metal poisoning
Fever	Warts
Gallbladder	Worms
Germ killer	Yeast infection

Garlic, called the "Stinking Rose" and "Russian Penicillin," is the world's second oldest medicine (after ephedra), and is still among the best. It is nature's antibiotic.

(*Garlic reportedly played a major role in the lives of the slaves who built Egypt's pyramids. The Egyptians believed garlic prevented illness and increased*

strength and endurance. They gave their
slaves a daily ration, and the slaves came
to revere the herb. Legend has it that
during the construction of one pyramid,
there was a garlic shortage. The Egyptians
cut the slaves' ration, and the slaves
rebelled, resulting in the world's first
recorded strike.)

GINGER

Bowels (spasms)	Heart palpitations
Childhood diseases	Indigestion
Circulation	Lung problems
Colds/coughs/flu	Morning sickness
Colitis	Motion sickness
Colon (spasms)	Nausea
Constipation	Nervous problems
Dizziness	Perspiration (promotes)
Fevers	Stomach (settles)
Gas pains	Sore throat
Headache	Whooping cough

Ginger is excellent for the respiratory system, effective as a cleansing agent through the bowels, kidneys, and the skin.

GINKGO

Alertness	Impotence
Alzheimer's	Longevity
Anxiety attacks	Memory loss
Attention span	Mental clarity
Brain function	Mood swings
Circulation	Shock
Depression	Senility
Equilibrium	Strokes
Hearing	Tinnitus
Heart problems	Vertigo
	Visual acuity

This plant's main use is said to be extending functional life. Ginkgo is reportedly an herb of longevity. It has been termed as a living fossil, having survived for thousands of years. It reportedly increases mental alertness and memory significantly, increases tissue oxidation and improves vital nutrients being delivered to the body tissues. It also improves ear problems as it improves blood flow to the nerves of the inner ear.

GINSENG

Age spots	Inflammation
Anemia	Liver diseases
Appetite	Longevity
Bleeding (internal)	Menopause
Blood diseases	Mental vigor
Depression	Nausea
Digestion	Nervousness
Drug antidote	Physical vigor
Endurance	Radiation protection
Euphoria (induces)	Sexual stimulant
Fatigue (banishes)	Stress
Fevers	Ulcers
Hemorrhage	Vomiting

In the Orient, Ginseng is known as the "King of the Herbs." It stimulates the entire body. It is considered a "cure-all" herb and reportedly slows down the aging process. It also reportedly improves vision and hearing activity. Ginseng acts as an antidote to various types of drugs and toxic chemicals, and is said to protect the body against radiation.

GOLDEN SEAL

Antibiotic
Antiseptic
Bleeding (internal)
Bowel problems
Bronchitis
Colds/flu (stomach)
Colon inflammation
Contagious diseases
Coughs
Earaches
Fever
Gastritis
General cleanser
Gonorrhea
Gun diseases
Hay fever
Herpes

Infections
Inflammation
Insulin, natural
Intestines
Morning sickness
Mouth sores
Poison ivy/oak
Ringworm
Scarlet fever
Sinus congestion
Skin disorders
Syphilis
Thyroid
Tonsillitis
Typhoid fever
Urinary problems
Venereal disease

Golden seal is considered king of all herbs for the Mucous Membranes, and as a natural antibiotic it stops infection and kills poisons in the body. It is ranked one of the best medicinal aids in the herbal kingdom.

GOTU KOLA

Age spots	Mental problems
Aging	Nervous breakdown
Blood purifier	Pituitary gland
Concentration	Schizophrenia
Depression	Senility
Fatigue	Stamina
Longevity	Tonic
Memory	Vitality

Gotu Kola is known as the "memory herb." It also acts to prevent aging, and is a mild tranquilizer. It is considered one of the best herbal nerve tonics. "Two capsules a day will keep old age away."—Health Handbook, Louise Tenney, M.H.

HAWTHORN

Adrenal weakness	Hardening of arteries
Angina pectoris	Heart disease
Arrhythmias	Hypertrophy
Arteriosclerosis	Hypoglycemia
Blood clots	Insomnia

Cardiac symptoms	Rheumatism
Congestive heart failure	Sleeplessness
Enlarged heart	Stress

Hawthorn is known as the "heart herb." Studies have shown that it is excellent for both the prevention and treatment of coronary heart disease when used on a regular basis. The Hawthorn tree i s regarded as sacred because the crown of thorns placed on the head of Christ was of its origin.

HOPS

Alcoholism (curbs desire)	Hoarseness
Anxiety	Hysteria
Appetite (stimulates)	Insomnia
Bed-wetting	Morning sickness
Delirium	Nervousness
Dizziness	Pain
Earaches	Sexual desires
Gas	(excessive)
Headaches	Worms (expels)

Hops has a sedative effect on the body. Fill a muslin pillow with it to help provide non drug-induced sleep. Has been known to calm the nerves and prevent nightmares. It is a natural preservative.

HORSETAIL

Bladder problems	Nails (brittle)
Circulation	Nose bleeds
Glandular disorders	Skin rashes
Hair (falling out/split ends)	Urinary problems

Horsetail is especially good for lower tract infections. Research indicates that fractured bones heal faster if horsetail is taken. Horsetail reportedly kills eggs of parasites and dissolves tumors.

HYDRANGEA

Backache	Inflammation
Bladder Infections	Kidney stones/problems
Calcium deposits	Pain
Gallstones	Scurvy
Gout	Urinary problems

Hydrangea reportedly removes bladder stones and the pain caused by them. It is helpful in preventing the formation of gravel and will help deposits pass through the urethra from the kidneys to the bladder. It also helps correct bed-wetting. Hydrangea reportedly contains curative principles second to none in nature.

JOJOBA

Abrasions	Hair moisturizer
Acne	Hair (shine/body)
Athletes foot	Mouth sores
Chapped skin	Pimples
Cuts	Scalp (dry)
Dandruff	Seborrhea
Dry skin	Warts
Hair conditioner	Wrinkles
Hair loss	

Jojoba was used by the Indians to promote hair growth. It helps cleanse and moisturize the scalp, and is helpful whether scalp is dry or oily.

JUNIPER

Abrasions	Incontinence
Adrenal glands	Infections
Bladder problems	Insect bites
Bleeding	Kidney infections
Bright's disease	Leukorrhea
Bursitis	Mucus
Colic	Snakebites
Contagious diseases	Tuberculosis
Fungal infections	Uric acid
Hair loss	Urinary problems
Hay Fever	Worms

Juniper is an excellent blood cleanser and diuretic. It prevents crystallization of uric acid in the kidneys.

KAVA KAVA

Anxiety	Nervousness
Fatigue	Spasms
Insomnia	Vaginitis

Kava Kava is an excellent sleep promoter and muscle relaxant.

KELP

Adrenal gland
Arteries (cleans)
Complexion
Digestion (poor)
Eczema
Energy
Fatigue
Fingernails
Gallbladder
Glands (enlarged)
Goiter

Hair loss
Kidneys
Lead poisoning
Morning sickness
Nervousness
Obesity
Radiation
Thyroid gland
Vitality (low)
Water retention

Kelp, is a product of the ocean, and contains many elements that are vital to the body. Kelp has the ability to neutralize wastes from the body fluids to be more easily discharged from the body.

LICORICE

Addison's disease
Adrenals (exhaustion)
Age spots

Drug withdrawal
Emphysema
Endurance

Arthritis (natural cortisone)	Female complaints
Asthma	Food poisoning
Blood cleanser	Hoarseness
Bronchial congestion	Hypoglycemia
Chills	Phlegm (expels)
Cushing's disease	Throat (sore)
Dizziness	Tonic
Dropsy	Voice

Licorice is known as the "voice herb." It also contains a natural hormone that will replace cortisone. It stimulates adrenal function without depleting the adrenals. **Do not take in large dosages however.**

LOBELIA

Allergies	Food poisoning
Asthma (acute/attacks)	Hay fever
Blood poisoning	Insomnia
Bronchitis	Lock jaw
Catarrh	Lung problems
Childhood diseases	Nerve relaxant
Colds	Palsy
Colic	Pneumonia

Congestion
Contagious diseases
Convulsions
Cough
Epilepsy

Scarlet fever
Spasms
Syphilis
Tonsillitis
Whooping cough

Lobelia is reportedly the most powerful relaxant in the herb kingdom. It has a genuine effect on the whole system. It contains a substance called lobeline, the action of which resembles that of nicotine. Thus this herb is most helpful in stopping smoking, because it decreases the desire for tobacco.

MARSHMALLOW

Asthma
Bed-wetting
Bladder
Bronchial infection
Catarrh
Cough, dry
Diabetes
Dysentery

Emphysema
Eyes (inflammation)
Gangrene
Gravel
Kidney problems
Lactation
Lung congestion
Urinary tract infections

Marshmallow is very soothing for any sore or inflamed part of the body. It will enrich the milk of nursing mothers and at the same time increase milk flow. It also works as a natural fiber to regulate bowel activity.

MILK THISTLE

Alcoholism	Hemorrhage
Chemotherapy	Hepatitis
Cirrhosis of liver	Jaundice
Convulsions	Kidney problems
Delirium	Liver damage
Depression	Radiation
Epilepsy	Snake bites
Fatty deposits	Spleen congestion

Milk Thistle is an antioxidant and free radical scavenger. It protects and rejuvenates the liver.

MULLEIN

Allergies	Breathing problems
Baby rashes	Bronchitis

Colds, coughs	Mucous membranes
Croup	Mumps
Dysentery	Pleurisy
Emphysema	Pneumonia
Insomnia	Respiratory problems
Joints (swollen)	Tuberculosis
Lung problems	Warts
Lymphatic problems	

Mullein has numerous uses, but one of the main uses is the treatment of lung disease. It is also excellent in the treatment of a wide range of respiratory problems.

OREGON GRAPE

Acne	Herpes
Appetite stimulant	Lymph glands
Blood conditions	Psoriasis
Bronchitis	Skin diseases
Digestive problems	Syphilis
Eczema	Urinary problems

Oregon grape is considered an excellent blood purifier and liver cleanser.

PARSLEY

Allergies	Kidney problems
Bladder infections	Liver
Blood builder/cleanser	Lumbago
Breath freshener	Prostate
Digestive disorders	Rheumatism
Dropsy	Thyroid
Gallbladder problems	Venereal disease
Gas	Water retention

Parsley is an excellent kidney cleanser. It is also a slow and gentle diuretic. As this herb acts as a laxative (although gentle), it **should not be used during pregnancy.**

PASSION FLOWER

Convulsions	Insomnia
Depression	Menopause
Epilepsy	Nervous breakdown
Eye strain/tension	Neuralgia
Fevers	Restlessness
Hot flashes	Seizures
Insomnia (chronic)	Vision (dimness)

Passion flower resembles the Crown of Thorns given to Jesus of Nazareth and was reportedly the symbol of the crucifixion during the early seventeenth century. It is known for its ability to aid in nervous disorders, and can also be useful to those who do not want to be dependent on synthetic sleeping pills and tranquilizers.

PEPPERMINT

Appetite
Bowel spasms
Chills
Colds
Colic
Constipation
Convulsions
Cramps, stomach
Digestive aid
Dizziness
Fainting
Fever
Flu
Gas
Headaches
Heartburn
Insomnia
Mental depression
Morning sickness
Motion sickness
Mouth sores
Nausea
Seasickness
Sore throat
Stomach spasms
Vomiting

Peppermint oil brings oxygen into the blood. It cleans and strengthens the entire body. It can be used for convulsions and spasms in children. The whole family can benefit from this herb, therefore, it is a good herb to have in the house.

PSYLLIUM

Colitis	Hemorrhage
Colon Cleanser	Intestinal tract
Constipation (prevents)	Ulcers
Diarrhea	Urinary tract

Psyllium lubricates, supplies bulk, and heals the intestines and colon. It strengthens the tissues and restores tone. Is reportedly good for auto-intoxication which can cause many diseases.

RED CLOVER

Acne	Skin diseases
Blood cleanser	Spasms
Cancer	Syphilis

Childhood diseases	Toxins
Leukemia	Vaginal irritations
Liver congestion	Whooping cough

Red Clover is useful as a nerve tonic and as a sedative for nervous exhaustion. Mixed with honey and water, it can be used as a cough syrup. It has been used as an antidote for cancer. Is a useful herb for children because of mild effect on the body.

RED RASPBERRY

After-birth pains	Hemorrhoids
Bowel problems	Labor pains
Breast feeding discomfort	Lactation
Bronchitis	Menstruation
Canker sores	Morning sickness
Childbirth	Nausea
Cholera	Pregnancy (entire
Colds/flu	time)
Constipation	Stomach
Diarrhea	Teething
Female organs	Uterus, prolapsed
Fevers	Vomiting

Red Raspberry is known as the "pregnancy herb." It strengthens the uterus wall, helps in nausea, helps prevent hemorrhage, reduces pain, and eases childbirth. It is a wonderful herb to use for children with colds, colic, diarrhea, stomachache, and fever, and for children simply in a "weakly" state.

SAGE

Baldness	Memory (improves)
Brain (stimulates)	Mouth sores
Bladder infections	Night sweats
Blood infections	Parasites
Gravel	Sore throat (gargle)
Gums (sore)	Teeth cleanser
Hair growth/tonic	Tonsillitis
Lactation (stops)	Yeast infections

Sage was used anciently as a staple remedy in the home and was thought to save and prolong life. It has benefited some in some types of insanity. Good for mental exhaustion.

ST. JOHNS WORT

After-birth pains	Hysteria
Bed-wetting	Insomnia
Bites, insect	Melancholy
Blood purifier	Nervous conditions
Breasts, caked	Palsy
Depression	Skin problems
Diarrhea	Spasms
Dysentery	Tumors
Hemorrhaging	Worms

St. Johns' Wort has been touted as the herbal prozac. It is used as an anti-depressant for disturbed people, has a sedative effect, is used for neuralgia, anxiety, and nervous tension. It also acts to remove tumor growths. **One should avoid strong sunlight while taking this herb.**

SARSAPARILLA

Age spots	Poison antidote
Blood purifier	Psoriasis
Hot flashes	Ringworm

Joint aches	Sexual problems
Hormone regulator	Skin diseases
Impotence	Skin parasites
Physical debility	Urinary problems
Poison antidote	Worms

Sarsaparilla is valuable when used as a glandular balancer. It contains the male hormone, testosterone, and progesterone, another valuable hormone produced by the ovaries in the female. It is a natural steroid.

SAW PALMETTO

Bladder diseases	Infertility
Breast (enlarge)	Nerves
Bright's disease	Obesity
Catarrhal problems	Reproductive
Glands	organs
Frigidity	Sex stimulant
Hormone regulation	Weight (increase)

Saw Palmetto is useful in all wasting diseases. Diseases of both male and female reproductive organs have been helped by

Saw Palmetto. This herb reportedly increases the size of the breasts of women of childbearing age.

SENNA

Breath, bad	Obesity
Biliousness	Pimples
Constipation	Skin diseases
Gallstones	Sores, mouth
Gout	Worms

Senna is a powerful laxative that increases the intestinal peristaltic movements. This herb should always be taken with other herbs such as ginger or fennel to prevent bowel cramps. **Senna should not be used in cases of inflammation of the stomach.**

SPIRULINA

Allergies	Liver disease
Appetite (decrease)	Poisoning (heavy
Blood cleanser	metal)

Blood pressure (regulates) Rejuvenation
Diseases (chronic)   Senility
Energy   Tonic
Food supplement   Weight reduction

Spirulina is known as a miracle food. It is the highest source in the world of Beta carotene and vitamin B-12. It has four times the protein of beef. It is a complete food but is lacking in carbohydrates. It is beneficial for any and all ailments that exist.

STEVIA

Addictions   Sugar substitute
Food cravings   Weight reduction

Stevia is a natural herbal sweetener that is claimed to be fifty to sixty times sweeter than sugar. It is non-toxic and safe to use. Stevia is also non-caloric, so when used for baking (other uses), it holds down the extra calories that sugar would have provided. It is safe to use even in severe cases of sugar imbalance.

UVA URSI

Bed-wetting	Nephritis
Bladder infections	Pancreas
Cystitis	Piles
Dysentery	Spleen
Gallstones	Uric acid
Gravel	Urinary disorders
Kidney problems	Vaginal discharge

Uva Ursi strengthens the urinary passages. It can be used as an antiseptic for kidney and bladder infections. Added to a hot bath, this herb is good for after childbirth, inflammations, hemorrhoids, and skin infections. It also stimulates the uterus to contract. **Pregnant women should not take it.**

VALERIAN

Alcoholism	Insomnia
Bladder problems	Muscle spasms
Bronchial spasms	Nervous
Convulsions	breakdown

Drug addiction   Shock
High blood   Spasms
Hysteria   Worms (expels)

Valerian is a strong nervine. When used as a tranquillizer, it leaves one feeling refreshed rather than sluggish. It is recommended for short-term use and should not be used by children.

WILD YAM

After-birth pain   Morning sickness
Birth control   Nerves
Dysmenorrhea   Ovarian pain
Exhaustion   Pregnancy
Female problems   Spasms
Menstrual cramps   Stomach
Miscarriage   Urinary problems

Wild Yam has a potent tonic effect on the uterus when taken throughout pregnancy. It has also been used for those with exhausted adrenals. It is good for nausea in pregnant women. It relieves cramps in the region of the uterus during the last trimester of pregnancy. This herb also expels gas from the stomach and bowels.

YARROW

Bladder problems
Blood cleanser
Bowels, hemorrhage
Bursitis
Chicken Pox
Diarrhea (infants)
Falling hair
Fevers
Flu
Hysteria
Lungs (hemorrhage)
Lungs
Nipples (sore)
Nose bleeds
Pleurisy
Pneumonia
Smallpox
Sweating
   (promotes)
Throat (sore)
Urine retention
Yeast infection

Yarrow is used to help regulate the function of the liver, acts as a blood cleanser, opens the pores to permit free perspiration for elimination of waste, and helps to clean the blood of uric acid. It usually breaks up a cold within twenty-four hours. It will tone up the entire system.

YELLOW DOCK

Acne
Arsenic poisoning
Blood disorders
Cancer
Constipation
Ear infections
Eczema
Eyelids (ulcerated)
Fevers
Hay fever
Hives
Itching
Leukemia
Pregnancy
Skin problems
Sores
Stamina
Stomach problems
Swellings
Thyroid glands
Varicose veins
Venereal disease
Vitality (lack of)
Worms

Yellow Dock is an excellent blood cleanser, tonic, and builder. It will tone up the entire system.

YOHIMBE

Aphrodisiac
Athletic formula
Blood pressure (lowers)
Body builder
Impotency
Sex stimulant

Yohimbe is a natural sexual stimulant/aphrodisiac without the negative side effects. It is a hormone stimulant and a strong aphrodisiac affecting both male and female impotency. It dilates the blood vessels of the skin and mucous membranes, bringing the blood closer to the surface of the sex organs and simultaneously lowering blood pressure.

Caution: Yohimbe should never be taken if the blood pressure is normally low or at the same time as foods or substances containing tyramine which is an amino acid found in liver, cheese and red wine. This herb should also be avoided if one has high blood pressure or heart problems.

YUCCA

Addison's disease	Gall bladder
Arthritis	Gout
Bursitis	Rheumatism
Cataracts	Skin irritations
Colitis	Urethritis
Detoxifier	Venereal disease

Yucca has been used for almost everything from making clothes to medical applications. Scientists have discovered that Yucca roots contain natural substances which are similar to steroids such as cortisone. It reduces inflammation of the joints and is primarily used for arthritic and rheumatoid conditions. When it is chopped up in water, it makes a natural lather and is an effective soap substitute.

The herbs/foods from God's Garden that we have explored in this chapter were all designed, by the master, to aid the body in some way. Space would not permit me to list all of the uses of these herbs. I have listed what I feel are some of the most important ones. These foods are your key to good health, vitality, and well-being.

"Your nutrition is in your hands! You must make sure that the foods you are choosing are the best you can buy in order to take care of your body. Remember that this is the one body you will have while you are still living on this earth... We are standing in faith for our healing but continue to put the same destructive, devitalized, dead foods into our bodies... Healing is promised in God's word if we obey His statutes. There are definite statutes in the Bible regarding what we put in our mouths... God will not bypass the laws that He set up and grant believers divine healing as long as they continue to bring illness upon themselves by completely ignoring and/or abusing His nutritional laws!"—Zoe Christian Fellowship, Los Angeles.

"My people are destroyed for lack of knowledge: because thou hast rejected knowledge, I will also reject thee..."

Education is the key.

Caution: Do not try to self diagnose and treat yourself for any ailment. Consult a qualified health care practitioner before beginning any herbal program.

Let us now take a look at more common foods from God's garden.

5

Common Foods
From
God's Garden

CHAPTER FIVE

Common Foods From God's Garden

*N*ot only are these foods that God created for us to enjoy readily available for us to purchase, but we can also grow some of them in our own gardens. Of course, we could also grow some of the foods about which we talked in chapter four. Some of us do, such as the all-powerful apple, aloe vera, alfalfa sprouts, cranberries, dandelion, garlic, parsley, and raspberries.

When these foods are grown organically and eaten in their natural state—raw, they contain nutrients that are healing and supply live, active nourishment to the body. When juiced, and sometimes properly combined with other juices, they are even more nourishing, because they can be quickly digested, assimilated and eliminated.

However, when these foods are grown in devitalized soil or cooked (unless lightly steamed), their nutritional value is greatly diminished or lost completely.

The nutritional value of these foods also depends on how they are combined in the body. If foods are improperly combined and not digested properly, they putrefy, and this putrefaction spills over into the blood stream that flows to all parts of the body—affecting the entire body.

Even if you eat the best foods—raw and organically grown—if they are not properly combined and digested, they are harmful to the body.

(We shall briefly discuss proper food combining in Chapter Six.)

Fruits

Apricot
Banana
Blackberries
Blueberries
Boysenberries
Cantaloupe
Cherries
Cranberries
Currants
Date
Elderberries
Fig
Gooseberries
Grapefruit
Grapes
Guava
Honeydew
Kiwi
Kumquat
Lemon
Lime
Mango
Nectarine

Orange
Peach
Pear
Persimmon
Pineapple
Plum
Pomegranate
Prune
Raisin
Raspberries
Strawberries
Tangelo
Tangerine
Tomato
Watermelon

Vegetables

Artichoke
Asparagus
Bamboo Shoot
Bell Pepper
Beet
Bok Choy
Broccoli
Brussels Sprout
Cabbage
Carrot
Cauliflower
Celery
Chive
Collard
Corn
Cucumber
Dandelion
Eggplant
Endive
Green Bean
Kale
Leek

Lettuce
Mushroom
Mustard
Okra
Onion
Parsnips
Peas, fresh
Radish
Rutabaga
Spinach
Sprouts
Squash
Swiss Chard
Turnip
Watercress
Zucchini

Let us now explore some of the benefits of these foods to the body.

Fruits are the cleansers of the body. They are especially beneficial when juiced. However, they should be eaten/drunk in their raw state. Vegetables are the builders and regenerators of the body.

When the whole fruit or vegetable is eaten in its raw, natural state, the fibers from these products act as an intestinal broom during the peristaltic activity of the intestines. Fiber from fruits and vegetables contain the atoms and molecules that are essential nutritional elements our bodies need.

When fruits and vegetables are juiced, extracting the fiber, they are more easily and quickly digested and assimilated, sometimes in a matter of minutes. And...there is very little effort and exertion of the digestive system.

Some nutritionists believe that when juices are extracted from fresh-raw fruits and vegetables, they are capable of furnishing the tissues and cells of the body with the nutritional enzymes and elements they need, and in the manner in which they can be most readily assimilated and digested.

Asparagus. An effective diuretic (especially when it is juiced and combined with carrot juice). It is also beneficial in cases of kidney disfunctions, anemia, and as a regulator of glandular troubles.

Beets. Reportedly help to build red corpuscles and tone the blood. Also effective as a liver cleanser.

Cabbage. Ulcers have reportedly responded well to this vegetable (especially when juiced). Cabbage also has wonderful cleansing and reducing properties. It has high sulphur, chlorine and iodine content.

Carrot. Richest source of Vitamin A. Also supplies Vitamins B, C, D, E, G, and K. Helps promote appetite and is an aid to digestion. Raw carrot juice has been used for ulcers, cancerous conditions, eye problems, intestinal and liver diseases. (These are just a few of the many uses of this vegetable.)

Celery. Contains high percentage of vital organic sodium that plays an important role in the physiological processes of the body. One of the most important is the maintenance of the fluidity of the blood and lymph—preventing their becoming too thick. Necessary in the generation and functions of digestive fluids. It contains potassium, sodium, calcium, phosphorus, and chlorine.

Cucumber. Is probably the best natural diuretic known to man. It secretes and promotes the flow of urine. It also contributes to hair growth, aids the conditions or high or low blood pressure, and pyorrhea. Is most helpful in preventing the splitting of the nails and falling out of the hair.

Dandelion. A valuable tonic. Counteracts hyperacidity and helps normalize the system. It is high in potassium, calcium, magnesium, iron, and sodium.

Endive. Rich source of Vitamin A. Good for liver and gall bladder disfunctions. Has elements of which the optic system is constantly in need. According to Dr. Norman W. Walker in his book, <u>Fresh Vegetable and Fruit Juices</u>, by adding endive juice to the juices of other vegetables such as parsley, carrot, and celery, the optic nerve can be nourished, bringing amazing results in correcting eye problems. Reportedly, one to two pints daily of this combination has been known to correct eye problems in a few months—to the point where normal vision was restored, eliminating the need for glasses.

Lettuce. Contains iron (the most active element in the body) and magnesium. It also contains phosphorus, potassium, sulphur. Contributes to healthy skin and hair and gastric disturbances.

Mustard Greens. Valuable to the body if eaten raw in salads or juiced. High content of sulphur and phosphorus. Mustard is also high in organic oxalic acid that aids the peristaltic action of the body. If cooked, however, Dr. Norman Walker says the oxalic acid becomes inorganic and is, therefore, harmful to the system. This is also true with kale, collard, and spinach, says Dr. Walker.

Onions. Build body physically. Is the sister herb to garlic—just less pungent.

Potato. When eaten raw, this vegetable supplies natural digestible sugars. However, when it is cooked the sugar turns to starch. Is valuable in skin blemishes, and has been known to aid emphysema victims. **The Sweet Potato.** Contains one-third more natural sugars than the "Irish" potato, three times more calcium, twice as much sodium, more than twice as much silicon, and more than four times as much chlorine. Choose carefully, as they are readily spoiled by bruises and decayed spots.

Radish. Contains potassium, sodium, iron and magnesium. Helpful in restoring the mucous membranes to their normal state. When juiced, should be combined with carrot juice, as it is too strong alone.

Spinach. Vital to the digestive tract, the small and large intestines. Wonderful for cleansing, reconstruction and regeneration of the intestinal tract. Also helps to prevent pyorrhea. Source of Vitamins C and E. Is often associated with laxatives because of its high content of oxalic acid. Spinach should never be cooked, because the organic oxalic acid will then become inorganic and may form oxalic acid crystals in the kidneys.

Tomatoes. Contain citric, malic, and some oxalic acid. These acids are beneficial in the processes of metabolism. Rich in sodium, calcium, potassium, and magnesium. If cooked, kidney and/or bladder stones may result—especially if eaten with starches and/or sugars.

Sprouts. Bean sprouts are full of vitamins and minerals and are edible raw. Great in salads. Can be sprouted at home. Mung beans are especially good for sprouting. You can also sprout whole peas, soybeans, lentils, and other small legumes. Just be sure the beans are intended for sprouting or cooking, not for planting, or they may have been treated with an insecticide or fungicide.

String Beans (green beans). Excellent for diabetes. (One cupful of string bean tea is reportedly equivalent to one unit of insulin.) Some nutritionists believe that, when combined, string bean and Brussels sprouts juices contain elements which supply the body with a natural form of insulin that enhances the pancreatic functions.

Turnip Greens. High in calcium. Aids bone structure, especially for growing children—or anyone with softening of the bones, when combined with the juice of carrots and dandelion. Also contains potassium. Has been known to aid the condition of hemorrhoids when combined with carrot and spinach juice.

Needless to say, eating these foods raw is the key to obtaining their maximum benefits to the body. So...instead of serving up a "pot of greens," a mustard, collard, spinach, kale, and turnip salad would be the healthy thing to do....?

Let us now look at a few simple keys to proper food combining.

6
FOOD COMBINING

CHAPTER SIX

Food Combining

Proper food combining is essential to good digestion. Improper food combining can cause all kinds of trauma to the body. In addition to improper digestion, it can cause fermentation in the colon, heartburn, gas, constipation, and the formation of toxins and poisons that can contribute to the formations of many abnormal conditions in the body, with some of these conditions eventually becoming life-threatening.

It is estimated that approximately one-half of the population in the United States is medically classified as chronically ill.

Do you suffer from, or know anyone who suffers from indigestion, heartburn, tiredness, aching joints, headaches, constipation, allergies, obesity, diabetes, high blood pressure, yeast infections, colds, bad breath, junk food cravings, sugar cravings...?

(Only a sick body craves sick food, and sick food will create a sick body. A healthy body does not want junk. The healthy body loves fresh vegetables, fruit and grains.)

If a food reaches a certain digestive organ and that food is not in the digestive condition it should be, it will not continue to digest. So what happens to it? It lies in the stomach and putrefies (rots). The longer the undigested food remains in the body the worse it gets. Whenever it does come out—if it comes out; it could still be adhering to the colon walls after many years—it will be foul!! This is especially so if you have ingested animal protein. After all, you are eating dead flesh, and rotting of dead flesh is a normal process.

It is a proven fact that people who eat properly (healthy foods in the right combinations) and have good digestion do not have foul-smelling bowel movements. If you do not believe this, try eating according to the guidelines in this book and see if your bowel movements will chase even you out of the bathroom. You might be pleasantly surprised.

Remember that the digestive tract begins at the mouth and ends at the rectum. If food putrefies anywhere between these two points, it affects the entire body.

Bad breath can be caused by infected gums or improper brushing of teeth—food left between gums or not brushing long or frequently enough. It can also be a sign of digestive problems. Breath mints provide only a temporary cover-up for this problem. One should get to the root of the problem and correct it.

Practicing Proper Food Combining

According to Louise Tanney in her book, <u>Nutritional Guide with Food Combining</u>, proper food combining begins with a glass of water and the juice of half a lemon the first thing in the morning. This cleans the stomach and aids the action of the liver.

Your body would appreciate waking up to something light after it has put itself into a natural fast while you were sleeping during the night. Fruit would be ideal to start your mornings, as it does not take much energy to digest. Remember, fruits are the cleansers of the body.

After your fruit meal, it is advisable that you not ingest anything else, except water or fruit juice, until noon. At this time, you should eat your biggest meal of the day.

According to Dr. Charles Czeisler of Harvard Medical School, as stated in Harvey and Marilyn Diamonds book, <u>Fit For Life II: Living Health,</u> the physiological functions of the body operate under cycles. He says there are three distinct cycles of approximately eight hours each. These cycles deal with the utilization of food. The first cycle is reportedly called the appropriation cycle. This cycle deals with eating and digestion, and is in effect from 12:00 noon to 8:00 p.m. The second cycle is called the assimilation cycle, and deals with absorption and use. It is in effect from 8:00 p.m. to 4:00 a.m. The third cycle, the elimination cycle, deals with the passing of body waste. This cycle is in effect from 4:00 a.m.-12:00 noon.

The appropriation cycle is when the the body is most capable of taking in and digesting food. Assimilation is more intense while we sleep, and it is during this cycle that the nutrients from our food and absorbed from the digestive tract are utilized. The elimination cycle is when the body has finished its work and rids itself of waste.

If we allow these cycles to function freely without interference, our systems will remain in a clean, healthy state rather than a toxic-laden, diseased one. This can be accomplished by practicing healthy eating habits.

Below are a few simple guidelines to follow for proper food combining:

1 Do not combine acids and starches.
2 Do not combine proteins and carbohydrates.
3 Do not combine proteins and acids.
4 Do not combine fats and proteins.
5 Do not eat more than one protein food at a meal.
6 Do not combine protein and starches.
7 Never have more than one starch at a meal.
8 Do not eat sugar with anything.
9 Never eat fruit with anything, not even other fruits, unless they are in the same category.

There must be a balance between alkaline-forming foods and acid-forming foods in the diet.

Acid foods include meat, fish, eggs, cheese, poultry, and nuts—except almonds

Alkaline foods include all vegetables and fruits (except plums and cranberries).

Vegetables - (Non-starch)

Asparagus
Bell pepper
Beets (top)
Broccoli
Brussels Sprouts
Cabbage
Cauliflower
Celery
Cucumber
Dandelion
Eggplant
Endive
Green Beans
Kale
Lettuce
Mushrooms
Okra
Onions
Peas, fresh
Radish
Spinach
Sprouts
Squash (except Banana, Hubbard)
Swiss Chard
Turnip Tops
Zucchini

Eat with: Fat, Starch, Mild Starch or (choose one) Protein Flesh, Protein Fat, Protein Starch, or Raw Tomato, Lemon.

Starch

Bread	Peanuts, raw
Cereal	Popcorn
Corn	Pumpkin
Crackers	Rice
Grains	Squash (Banana
Jerusalem Artichoke	Hubbard)
Lima Beans, fresh	Yams
Pasta	

Eat with: Fat, Non-Starch/Green Vegetables.

Protein Flesh

Beef	Pork
Chicken	Rabbit
Duck	Seafood
Egg	Turkey
Goose	Veal
Lamb	

If you feel you must eat from this category, eat with: Non-Starch/Green Vegetables.

Mild Starch
Beets   Rutabaga
Carrots   Turnips

Eat with: Non-Starch/Green Vegetables, Fat.

Protein Starch

Beans, dry   All Soy Products
Peas, dry

Eat with: Green Vegetables.

Protein Fat

Avocado   Olives
Cheese   Seeds
Nuts (except Chestnut   Sour Cream
   Peanut), Raw   Yogurt

Eat with: Fat, Non-Starch/Green Vegetables or Fruit.

Fat

Butter   Oil
Cream

Eat with: Starch, Non-Starch, Mild Starch
or Protein Fat.

Fruit Acid

Acerola Cherry   Lime
Apple, sour   Orange
Cranberry   Peach, sour
Currant   Pineapple
Grapefruit   Plum, sour
Grapes, sour   Strawberry
Kumquat   Tangerine
Lemon   Tomato

Eat Alone.

Fruit Sub-Acid

Apple, sweet   Blueberry
Apricot   Boysenberry
Blackberry   Cherry, sweet

Elderberry
Fig, fresh
Huckleberry
Kiwi
Mulberry

Nectarine
Peach, sweet
Pear
Plum
Raspberry

Eat Alone.

Fruit, Dried-Sweet

Apricot
Banana
Date
Fig

Pear
Pineapple
Prune
Raisin

Eat Alone.

Fruit, Fresh-Sweet

Banana
Black Currant
Mango

Papaya
Persimmon
Thompson Grape

Eat Alone.

Melons

Cantaloupe   Watermelon
Honeydew

Eat Alone.

If you ingest milk, drink it alone as a meal, and, according to Lee DuBelle, <u>Proper Food Combining Works</u>, nothing else should be ingested for the next twelve hours.

Other Factors to Consider.

- Never drink with meals. Drink at least fifteen minutes before or two hours after your meal.
- Never drink ice cold or too hot sub-stances. They shock the system.
- Never drink water from a tap where a water-softener is used. It is loaded with salt.
- Eat as early as possible in the evening to allow your meal to digest before retiring.

- Do not eat between meals. If you feel you must eat something, let it be fruit.
- Keep meals simple. We have been taught that a balanced diet is one providing many different foods at one meal. Not so—the less the better.
- Do not eat if you are tired, worried, fearful or angry.
- Do not eat if you are cold or too hot.
- Do no eat when you have a fever or if you are in pain.
- Do not eat when you are not hungry. A certain time of day has nothing to do with whether your body needs food.
- Do not lie down immediately after eating a meal, and especially if you are tired. You cold die in your sleep if your food has not had time to digest and combustion, caused by indigestion, presses against the heart so hard that it stops beating.
- Never exercise immediately after eating.
- Avoid salad bars. Preservatives will have probably been put on the vegetables so they will look nice and fresh.

I do hope this chapter on food combining has been helpful to you.

Now let us take a look at herbs and drugs and how they work in the body. Is there a comparison?

7

HOW GOD'S MEDICINE
AND MAN'S MEDICINE
WORK
IN THE BODY
(The comparison)

CHAPTER SEVEN
How God's Medicine And Man's Medicine Work In The Body

If you were sick and man stood on one side of you offering you his drugs and God stood on the other offering you his herbs, which would you accept?

Dumb question, right? We all know which offering you would accept. So I ask you now to think about herbs and drugs and to which you would rather entrust your body when it is sick.

The comparison? There is none. God made the herbs; man makes drugs. It is as simple as that. Man could never match God in anything he does. Of course, man knows this, and he is doing the best he can with what he knows. Education is the key factor here. Open-mindedness could also be a plus in this analogy of these two things that were designed for the same purpose, and yet are so different in so many ways.

HOW HERBS WORK IN THE BODY

1 They cleanse our temples (bodies).
2 They regulate the system.
3 They are nutritional.
4 They raise the energy level.
5 They stimulate the body's immune system to ward off illness and disease.
6 They keep our temples fit with energy to spare.

Cleansing the body. The body was built with safeguards and healing powers within it. When we are cut, the body goes to work, trying to repair the damage. When we are invaded by an illness, the body's immune system is alerted and starts to defend against the illness. Waste products are gathered and eliminated from the body daily. The body works constantly to cleanse and heal itself. Herbs help, rather than interfere, with this cleansing, healing, and eliminating process.

There is an herb for every "dis-ease" (disease) with which the body might be afflicted. Down through the ages, much has been written about herbs and their ability to cleanse the body and bring it back into harmony and health naturally.

Regulating the system. In addition to helping the body cleanse, herbs also strengthen and normalize the glands. Sometimes it is surprising to find that the same herb can be used for too much hormone or for too little hormone or for decreasing or increasing the appetite. This ceases to be surprising when we understand that herbs regulate and tone the glands to return them to their normal function.

Nourishing the body. Herbs nourish and build the body. They are valuable, natural sources of vitamins, minerals, and other nutrients/ substances that the body uses to affect repair and maintenance, and are considered food for the body. Wholesome, non-poisonous herbs are special foods that help to nourish, build, and repair the tissues of the body. They are valuable sources of natural medicine that have a history of curative powers when used properly. Many times, a weak or sick body will accept nourishment from an herb when other foods are rejected or unassimilated.

Raising the energy level. Herbs stimulate the energy levels within the body, adding stamina and strength to enable the body to function properly as it meets the challenges and rigors of daily living. Herbs also enable the body to have increased energy, if sick, to heal itself.

Stimulating the body's immune system. A compromised immune system leaves the body susceptible to illness and disease. A weak immune system is manifested in many ways—frequent colds, infections, fatigue, and irritability. Often serious health problems arise that could easily become life-threatening, if the immune system is not rebuilt to the point where it is capable of defending the body. Herbs stimulate the immune system enabling it to fight off foreign invaders. They also help promote the body's natural good bacteria.

Keeping our temples fit with energy to spare. In this author's opinion, constipation is the chief reason for decreased energy and for many of the illnesses that plague our society today—and the chief reason for constipation is the consumption of improper foods.

Herbs work by way of the elimination organs: The colon (bowels), lungs (mucus), kidneys (urine), and skin (sweat). Each of these organs should eliminate approximately two pounds of waste per day. When they function properly, we have few health problems and energy to spare.

Devitalized/processed foods clog the system and keep the body totally constipated, causing the elimination system to lock up—thus, the body becomes tired and ill. The waste from the colon spills directly into the bloodstream, and the body becomes poisoned by its own waste.

Herbs, when combined with good food—fruits, vegetables, nuts, seeds, grains, beans, etc. as well as exercise, proper rest, pure water, fresh air, and positive thinking, will energize and expedite healing of the body's tissues, and cells.

Herring's law of cure states that, "All cure starts from within out and from the head down and in reverse order as the symptoms have appeared." In other words, when the body is healing itself, there is under way an acute stage of what previously occurred during the course of a disease process—the disease leaving the body in the reverse order in which it entered. The body feels sick first then it gets better.

Herbs go to work as soon as they enter the bloodstream. They fit everyone, from the fetus to the aged adult—even the animal kingdom. Sometimes, if there is an imbalance in the body, one might experience an allergic reaction to a substance in an herb, but, normally, if one experiences a reaction from an herb, it is usually because of toxic waste leaving the body via the bloodstream, not the herb itself. This reaction is called a "healing crisis." This is sometimes necessary in order to bring the body back to a state of physiological equilibrium —homeostasis.

The rule of thumb for getting well is: for every year we violate our bodies, it takes a month to get well—which means we get well eleven times faster than we got sick.

Once again, <u>diet is the key</u>. After all, nothing runs better than the fuel it uses.

Herbs are nature's remedy and have been put on this earth by an all wise Creator for man's use. There is an herb for every disease with which man can be afflicted.

The use of herbs is the oldest medical science in the world, and is, therefore, one of mankind's oldest forms of healing.

For thousands of years, mankind has turned to the herbs of the field as a source of healing power. Animals instinctively use them when they are sick. Even today millions of people throughout the world rely on natural medicine as their primary form of health care.

Thousands of people throughout North America have found through their own experience that herbs can help the body heal itself of many so-called incurable" diseases. They have also discovered that these natural substances do not build up residual effects with continued use, have no toxic side effects, and are safe when used as recommended.

The lives of many men, women, and children have been blessed for generations because of the many wonders of nature's herbs. Today's health-conscious public is now realizing that herbs can promote all-around better living through the attainment of better health.

Many people are failing to find answers to their problems through orthodox medicine. Modern medicine offers little or no help for cure of today's killer diseases, so people are looking for alternatives, because they are tired of the harmful side effects and the high cost of modern medicine. They feel that there must be a safer and less expensive way to achieve good health.

Herbs offer an attractive alternative because of their long history of safe use. Many religious traditions teach that herbs were provided by our Creator who prepared them to heal every affliction we might suffer. Others feel that herbs are part of getting back to "Mother Nature" and living more in harmony with the planetary system which supplies all of our other physical needs. Many feel that our bodies have evolved over thousands of years to utilize the elements found in plants for tissue growth and repair.

Whatever the reason, many people feel that these natural substances are superior to modern man's chemical medicines. It has been documented that medications kill over 100,000 people annually.

What would you do if your body were diseased and your doctor told you there was nothing else he/she could do for you? Would you begin making out your will and prepare to meet your maker? Or would you try to find an answer to your problem? After all, it is your body and your responsibility.

"Herbs are our heritage. (Genesis 1:29)." — Zoe Christian Fellowship.

"And God said, Behold, I have given you every herb bearing seed, which is upon the face of all the earth, and every tree, in the which is the fruit of a tree yielding seed; to you it shall be for meat."
Amen.

HOW DRUGS WORK IN THE BODY

The making of modern medicine is sometimes begun with natural substances extracted from medicinal plants. Research shows that when these isolated substances are removed from their natural base of balance/their wholistic state, to make drugs, they become harmful chemicals. Just as sugar becomes harmful to the system when it has been refined, the chemicals found in herbs become harmful "drugs." Because these isolated chemicals are not whole, they cannot restore the body to wholeness (especially when they are combined with synthetic substances). This is why we have so many side effects from prescribed medicines. They pose many hazards to the body such as contributing to kidney failure, liver damage, immune system depression, suicidal tendencies, and even death.

Every drug has some possible side effects. These side effects are greatly increased if a person has more than one ailment for which he/she is being treated.

In 1991, an Anti-inflammatory drug
was prescribed for an ailment my body was
experiencing at that time. I asked for a
listing of the side effects. There were forty-
six listed. Here are some of the things this
drug has the capability of doing to the body:

Cause dizziness
Cause severe stomach pain, cramping, or
  burning
Cause the body to emit bloody or black tarry
  stools
Cause one to have seizures
Cause one to faint
Cause one to have hive-like swellings on
  various parts of body
Cause breathing problems
Cause one to vomit material that looks like
  coffee grounds or blood
Cause severe headache with stiff neck
Cause crusting sores on lips
Cause cloudy or bloody urine
Cause forgetfulness
Cause hearing problems
Cause one to hallucinate

Cause mental depression
Cause high blood pressure
Cause nosebleeds
Cause numbness/tingling/pain in hands, feet
Cause painful or swollen glands
Cause sores to appear in mouth
Cause one to spit up blood
Cause swelling of face, feet, or lower legs
Cause one to gain weight rapidly
Cause vision problems

I was shocked when I read that list. I could not imagine anything that was designed to help the body had the potential to do so much harm to it.

Do you think I took that medicine? Not if I valued my life. I did and still do. I threw that medicine away but saved the bottle and the list of side effects to remind me of what might have happened to my body if I had not requested a list of the side effects and blindly taken the drug.

Just as this drug had so may side effects, so do many others. Some do not have the tendency to impose as many problems as others, but, in my opinion, any substance that creates problems in the body should be avoided.

Perhaps you should consider requesting a list of the side effects of any medication you might consider taking in the future. Look at the side effects and decide whether taking the drug would benefit or harm your body.

The choice is yours.

We must be constantly vigilant and continue to educate ourselves. Our lives may well depend on it.

EPILOGUE

Many drugs are dispensed to millions daily. Some medications do alleviate the symptoms of some ailments/diseases, but, unfortunately, they create other problems in the body. It has been documented that many people die from adverse reactions to these drugs annually.

Remember that herbs produce no side effects in the body and cause no adverse reactions—unless the herb is overused or the person is allergic to a substance in the herb.

(I am allergic to iodine, so I don't take herbs that contain that element. The adverse reactions in my body are always minor such as itching or a rash. When I discontinue the herb, the symptoms go away. If my body would accept iodine, I would definitely be taking, along with my Bilberry, two other herbs for the eyes that have reportedly helped to restore vision 100 percent. I am taking the slow route to

enjoying perfect vision again, but I am getting there—as evidenced by my visit to the optometrist who did not believe his machinery was working properly when it told him my new lenses needed less strength rather than more.)

No one wants to relinquish control of his/her own health, but most people are thoroughly confused because of the continuous onslaught of differing opinions of the so-called health experts. And to compound things, we are constantly told that we are incapable of determining what is best for our own health. We are expected to follow the advice of others blindly and without question. It is an expensive, and often detrimental, health choice.

As I often heard my father, Mr. Joe Ben Dumas, one of the smartest men I have ever had the pleasure of knowing, say, "Use you head, your own good common sense."

Modern drugs do often provide some form of relief. But that relief is only temporary, and that is mostly because the drugs target the symptoms that the person is experiencing, but do little—if anything at all—to address the underlying cause of the patient's pain or discomfort. The cause must be addressed and eliminated if the patient is to gain permanent or substantial relief. Herbs provide safer, better, less costly, and more effective healing options.

"And by the river upon the bank thereof, on this side and on that side, shall grow all trees...and the fruit thereof shall be for meat, and the leaf thereof for medicine." Ezekiel 47:12.

We don't expect God to come down from his throne to dispense His medicine to us, but we do know that he sometimes uses people to do His work for Him. I like calling myself "One of God's Little Herbal Helpers." There are quite a few of us around—and the number is growing as more and more people begin to take charge of their own health.

I do hope **God's Diet For His People** has been helpful and a blessing to you. Thank you for reading this book with an open mind and a desire to learn how to live a healthier and more gratifying life.

Some of you will accept the opinions and thoughts of this author, quotes and beliefs of others (or some of them at least) expressed in this book; some will not. It is your body, your health, and your choice. I wish you and yours the best of health.

May God bless.

Bibliography

The Holy Bible, Authorized King James Version.

Balch, James F., M. D. and Balch, Phyllis A., C.N.C., *Prescription for Nutritional Healing.* Avery Publishing Group, Inc., Garden City Park, New York, 1990.

Bashaw, Ed, *Life Abundantly.* Bashaw Life Center, Midlothian, Virginia, 1990.

Bumgarner, Marlene A., *the Book of Whole Grains.* St. Martin's Press, New York, N. Y., 1986.

Castleman, Michael, *The Healing Herbs.* Rodale Press, Emmaus, PA, 1991.

Diamond, Harvey and Marilyn, *Fit For Life II: Living Health.* Warner Books, Avenue of the Americas, New York, N. Y., 1989.

Dixon, Barbara M., L.D.N., R.D. with Wilson, Josleen, *Good Health for African Americans.* Crown Publishers, Inc., New York, N. Y., 1994.

DuBelle, Lee, *Proper Food Combining Works.* Phoenix, AZ, 1992.

Duke, James A., Ph.D., *Nature's Remarkable Healing Herbs—Pocket Guide.* Prevention Health Books.

Goldberg, Burton Group, *Alternative Medicine: The Definitive Guide.* Future Medicine Publishing, Inc., Puyallup, Wash-ington, 1994.

Ingram, Cass, Dr. with Gray, Judy K, M.S., *Eat Right To Live Long.* Cedar Graphics, Inc., Hiawatha, Iowa, 1989.

Jensen, Bernard, Ph.D., *The Chemistry of Man.* Bernard Jensen Enterprises, Escon-dido, CA, 1983.

Robbins, John, *Diet For A New America.* Stillpoint Publishing, Walpole, NH, 1987.

Morter, Dr. M. Ted, Jr., M.A., *Your Health...Your Choice.* Lifetime Books, Inc., Hollywood, FL, 1995.

Olsen, Cynthia B., *101 Ways To Use Tea Tree Oil—Handbook.* Kali Press, Pagosa Springs, CO, 1991.

Prevention Health Specials, *Healing Herbs.* Rodale Press, Emmaus, PA.

Prevention Magazine Health Books Editors, *Visual Encyclopedia Or Natural Healing.* Rodale Press, Emmaus, PA, 1991.

Ritchason, Jack, N.D., *The Little Herb Encyclopedia.* Woodland Health Books, Pleasant Grove, UT, 1995.

Tenney, Louise, M.H., *Health Handbook: A Guide to Family Health.* Woodland Books, Provo, UT, 1987.

Tenney, Louise, M.H., *Modern Day Plagues.* Woodland Books, Provo, UT, 1987.

Tenney, Louise, M.H., *Nutritional Guide With Food Combining.* Woodland Books, Pleasant Grove, UT., 1994.

Tenney, Louise, *Today's Herbal Health, 2nd Edition.* Woodland Books, Provo, UT., 1983.

Walker, Norman W., Dr., *Fresh Vegetable and Fruit Juices.* O'Sullivan Woodside & Company, Phoenix, AZ, 1981.

Other References

Flot, Barbara, Dr., Herbal Connection, Gardena, CA.

Herbal Connection South, Los Angeles, CA.

Zoe Christian Fellowship, Los Angeles, CA.

"And God said, Behold, I have given you every herb bearing seed, which is upon the face of all the earth, and every tree, in the which is the fruit of a tree yielding seed; to you it shall be for meat... And God saw every thing that he had made, and, behold, it was very good." Genesis 1:29 and 31.